TURN TOWARD

Mercy

EXPERIENCE
THE PASSION,
THE PRESENCE,
AND THE GLORY
OF GOD

THOM GARDNER

Bridge-Logos
Orlando, Florida 32822

Bridge-Logos

Orlando, FL 32822 USA

Turn Toward Mercy
by Thom Gardner

Library of Congress Catalog Card Number: 2006940407
International Standard Book Number 978-0-88270-334-2

G163.316.N.m612.35250

Contents

PART III MERCY: THE GLORY OF GOD

Battered Reeds and Smoldering Wicks

"BEHOLD, MY SERVANT WHOM I HAVE CHOSEN;
MY BELOVED IN WHOM MY SOUL IS WELL-PLEASED;
I WILL PUT MY SPIRIT UPON HIM,
AND HE SHALL PROCLAIM JUSTICE TO THE GENTILES.
HE WILL NOT QUARREL, NOR CRY OUT;
NOR WILL ANYONE HEAR HIS VOICE IN THE STREETS.
A BATTERED REED HE WILL NOT BREAK OFF,
AND A SMOLDERING WICK HE WILL NOT PUT OUT,
UNTIL HE LEADS JUSTICE TO VICTORY.
AND IN HIS NAME THE GENTILES WILL HOPE." (MATT 12:18-21)

A man and woman sit exhausted on opposite sides of the lawyer's table. A look of empty resignation overshadows their faces as they divide up the ruins of irreconcilable differences. There seems to be no other alternative—no other apparatus to maintain the integrity of their covenant. Both sink into leather-covered chairs loaded down with guilt and the weight of failed expectations. There seems to be nowhere else to go. They are like the man who lay helplessly by the pool of mercy waiting for someone to take him to the water. There was no help for them—no place of comfort. They are bruised and bent nearly flat under the burden of justice or injustice as the case may be. The light has been snuffed out.

BATTERED REEDS

We are surrounded by battered reeds and smoldering wicks. The battered reeds are those who have been crushed—flattened and bent nearly double. They have grown numb under the weight of offenses and unresolved conflicts, brittle with wounds—scored along a line and ready to be broken in two as a piece of glass. It may be that they are bent double by their own sin or the compulsive justice they would meet out to those who have sinned against them. Regardless of who bears the blame, they themselves bear the weight of it.

SMOLDERING WICKS

Smoldering wicks are those whose lamps are out of oil. Life and virtue have been poured out with no way to refill the lamp. Smoldering wicks are those whose lives are depleted—whose wick is out of oil with the last hint of smoke wafting into the air. The oil is the light and hope that keeps them moving. It and their lives have been used up and their lights nearly extinguished—their virtue nearly exhausted.

Together these present the picture of the need. They are the wounded and the weary—they are all around us—*they are us*.

A NEW REALM OF LIFE

There is a realm of power and sweetness pouring from the throne of God that overwhelms those living here at His footstool (Isaiah 66:1). There is a fragrance that draws us to the table of God's mercy. The Bible quotation above describes the rising of the "Servant" of God—the Messiah—Jesus Christ. God has placed His spirit, His character upon this Servant. Now we see the arising of His character We are entering a new realm and season in the life of those who follow Christ. This is a season more of character than charisma, one in which we are becoming the fragrance of Christ to the perishing (2 Corinthians 2:15). If we are to take part in this season of renewal it will be by coming to maturity and growing up to the Head of the body and by becoming what He is.

Battered reeds surround us in our personal lives and connections as well. They are the unforgiven and even the unrepentant. They are the ones we have written off and placed beyond the hope of even God's boundless grace. Jesus never wrote anyone off—they always had good credit at the mercy bank. In fact He went out of His way to find them, to touch them, to bring them to His table.

Jesus, the Anointed Servant of God, was Himself both the battered reed and the smoldering wick. He hung from His cross battered by the unjust and cruel blows of the very ones He loved so. He was perfect and sinless, deserving mercy more than any other ever born, though He never "cried out" (v. 19) for it. As Jesus denied Himself, healing life and anointing were crushed out of Him at Gethsemane like the olives that released their oil under the weight of that press.[1] In this crushing of self the very heart of God was released to the battered and depleted. He recognizes and agonizes with those who have been crushed as He was.

AS HE WAS, SO ARE WE...

The profile of the Servant is also the profile of the merciful—the ones through whom the world will see the heart of God, "because as He is, so also are we in this world" (1 John 4:17b). We who have been partakers of his divine salvation are also "partakers of the divine nature, having escaped the corruption that is in the world by lust" (2 Peter 1:4). Everything we need has been given to us in Christ. Therefore, with no need for vengeance or mere justice, we are free to extend mercy.

Like the Servant, we are children and servants of God who present no will of our own and who rely upon the One served. The word translated servant is *pais*, which means servant and child. Jesus was both child and servant of the Father. We can also give away something sweet because Daddy owns the candy store. We give to whoever is there.

As the Servant was, so are we the *loved* and *chosen* of God (v. 18). What could we need that even approaches that? This is the place of total safety and purpose. We are the delight of our Father—the ones in whom He takes particular pleasure just like we do with our own kids. If our Father loves us who can hurt us or threaten us?

Just as Jesus did, we are to proclaim the Father's heart of mercy, even to the Gentiles, those who in our lofty estimation don't deserve it. But then, if they deserved it, it would not be mercy, would it? We are the ones filled with His Spirit that demonstrates His approval to us and through us.

What must the battered and depleted of Jesus' day have seen in His eyes as He carried the heart of the Father to them? What did hookers and dishonest revenuers feel at his approach? Did they feel shame or hope? What do the battered and depleted see in our eyes? What do those who have hurt you—those whose markers you hold feel at your approach?

Perhaps the most telling question of all is, what do we feel at the approach of the Lord? What does the thought of His presence make us want to do? Are we running in fear or hiding in shame? Or do we feel invited to run into His arms?

We know about the work of the cross but have we truly accepted it? Has it defined us? Do we really believe it enough to fall into the embrace of the Father? Can we smell the fragrance of His aftershave as it were?

It is in His name that the gentiles hope. The "name" is the distillation of the character and heart of God. That name is love manifested through mercy. Mercy is the supreme source of hope for those who are battered and depleted. In the end, nothing else will bring peace to us but the name of God. In the name of God we are drawn to a table of grace rather than one of negotiation.

We see the Father's heart unfolded and displayed through His mercy. I do not pretend to know the heart of God perfectly, but I can see what it is like. I know it is mercy that is at the core of His heart—mercy that compels God to pour out His love and empty Himself to us, the battered reeds and smoldering wicks.

O Israel, hope in the LORD; For with the LORD there is mercy (Psalm 130:7, NKJV)

ENDNOTES

1 GETHSEM'ANE (geth-sem'a-ni; Gk. from Aram. "oil press") (From *The New Unger's Bible Dictionary*. Originally published by Moody Press of Chicago, Illinois. Copyright (c) 1988.)

PART ONE

Mercy

THE PASSION OF GOD

CHAPTER 1

An Unreasonable Love

One day as I was sitting with the Lord, I asked him a question: "Lord, what is mercy like?"

His response was immediate and a little surprising. The first words that came into my mind were, "*Mercy is like honeysuckle.*"

"What?! Honeysuckle?" I asked.

You see, I have had an on-and-off battle with honeysuckle vines for more than twenty years. They have grown in, through, and over the fences we built around our home to keep our little girls in the yard and off the road.

Our "little" girls are now grown and they have children of their own, but the honeysuckle vines continue to grow as an asymmetrical menace, taking over more and more territory each spring. In vain we have tried to put an end to their all-consuming growth. We've tried everything, including poison, and cutting, but nothing seems to work. The mission of the honeysuckle is to grow, and it keeps on growing relentlessly!

The problem with honeysuckle is that it doesn't respect things like neat fence lines and boundaries. It pays no attention to "the way things ought to be." It will even grow away from our neat hedges and fences into our neighbor's yards, completely obliterating all respectable limits. How are we supposed to know where to stop mowing the grass if we can't see where our property line ends? How can we maintain a neat piece of property without having reasonable order? There need to be clear and distinct lines!

Honeysuckle grows so well that it literally overwhelms the area in which it takes root, and it overtakes all other plant life, even the flowers and shrubs we plant. This kind of wild behavior doesn't sit well with us, because we humans don't like to lose control of anything.

We spend our time purposefully trying to make things fair and orderly by planting our vegetables and flowers in neat little rows. The honeysuckle vine, however, grows on wildly, seemingly out of control, and it overtakes and overshadows all forms of competition. It's like a B science fiction movie from the 1950s, "The Vine that Wouldn't Die."

In His response to me, the Lord was trying to show me something about the nature of mercy by comparing it to honeysuckle. He knew that my experience with this vine would enable me to understand His point. In effect He was saying that mercy, like honeysuckle, grows relentlessly in order to conquer all kinds of obstacles that result from our human relationships and limited human reason. It overwhelms our hearts like the vine overcomes my fences. Once mercy takes hold and winds its fragrant vines around our hearts and minds there is no argument against it, and all attempts to resist it are in vain.

Jesus was mercy-in-person when He walked on the earth. His life and ministry were very much like the honeysuckle that grows on our fence. Jesus, in His great mercy and love for humanity, was always saying unreasonable and seemingly scandalous things to reveal the truth to people. For example, He said, "Love your enemies…When someone gives you a hard time, respond with the energies of prayer, for then you are working out of your true selves, your God-created selves…In a word, what I'm saying is, Grow up. You're kingdom subjects. Now live like it. Live out your God-created identity. Live generously and graciously toward others, the way God lives toward you" (Matt 5:43-45, 48, MSG).

Like the strong and ubiquitous vines of the honeysuckle, mercy wraps itself around the hurts and wounds that control and condition our hearts toward God and one another. Oh, if only the honeysuckle of mercy could wrap itself around and join together a couple sitting at a lawyer's polished hardwood table dividing the spoils of their "irreconcilable differences." Oh, if only it would overwhelm the hatred and suspicion that causes us to walk on the other side of the street when we see one who has hurt us in the past—such mercy would cause us to forget the offense. Oh, if only we could see folk as God sees them—then our hearts would be stirred with deep compassion for them. This is the fruit of mercy's vine. Are we being too unrealistic or idealistic to believe that love really does cover a multitude of sins? (See 1 Peter 4:8.)

The answer is no. I submit that it is reasonable to believe in God's unreasonable love and mercy, because it is our only hope for healing all kinds of relationships—God-to-human and person-to-person.

God's unreasonable love and mercy, like the honeysuckle vine, always overwhelms my self-centeredness and personal rights in favor of displaying the very heart of God in the midst of the most difficult circumstances and conflicts. It is mercy, that unreasonable, wild honeysuckle vine that grows over the railings of heaven in order to reach humanity. In so doing, it displaces all kind of wounds stemming from betrayal and unfairness along with all the other intrusions that vie for our heart's attention and affections.

The honeysuckle of mercy, therefore, must keep on growing in my life, taking the place of my wretched and puny attempts at love. In our conversation the Lord reminded me that when I allow honeysuckle to take control of my yard, it also sends out a fragrance of unrivaled sweetness. This pleasant fragrance greets us each spring and reminds us of new life and hope.

The purpose for this book is to unveil God's unreasonable and fragrant love, which is so extravagantly expressed in His mercy. I call it "God's honeysuckle love." And about this wonderful love and mercy, God says, *"Let it grow!"* He wants it to overwhelm the fence rows and neatly manicured lines of our rational, controlled love. God's mercy is the nectar of heaven, and as it wraps itself around us, we become the "fragrance of Christ." (See 1 Cor. 2:15.)

This book reveals that mercy is the passion, the presence, and the very glory of God.

Finding a Safe Place

Then the LORD said, "Behold, there is a place by Me …" (Ex. 33:21).

In our minds and hearts we can establish a place that is just for communing with the Lord. It is a meeting place—a safe place where the Lord speaks to us through words, images, scriptures, thoughts and any other number of ways. Throughout this book, at the end of each chapter you'll need to go to your "safe place" of quietude to do the prayer and journaling exercises or "Turning Points."

Your safe place will be a place of meditation where you close your eyes and allow the Lord to interact with you. It is a place where you listen to Him speaking to your heart through your mind. You learn to trust and identify His voice as you listen to Him.

This safe place is one we see in our minds. I find that using a scriptural context for the safe place is very effective. As we read the scriptures the Lord frequently brings images to our minds. For example, what pictures come to mind when you read the words, "The Lord is my Shepherd, I shall not want…" (Psalm 23:1)? Do you see a shepherd holding a lamb or something similar? That can become a safe place for you where you have conversations with the Lord.

The Lord is waiting for you in the safe place of your mind and heart—a place where He will cover you with His presence and open His heart to you.

I've divided the book into three parts:

I. Mercy: The Passion of God (The What and Why of Mercy)

II. Mercy: The Presence of God (The Emblems of Mercy)

III. Mercy: The Glory of God (The Vehicle of Mercy for God's Glory)

As you read, you will follow God's invitation to Moses to come into the very glory of His heart and be consumed with all that consumes Him. On the mountain where Moses encountered God, the Father unveiled His heart through the instructions He gave to Moses with regard to creating a place for His habitation—the Tabernacle with all its furnishings, including *the Mercy Seat*.

David wrote, "O taste and see that the LORD is good; blessed is the man who takes refuge in Him! [Who is taken over and overwhelmed by the invasive and unreasonable love of the Father ...] (Psalm 34:8).

Turning Points

FEEL THE PASSION

Beloved ones, the Lord has loved you with a fragrant and unreasonable love. As you grow in this love and its fragrance permeates your life, you will send its aroma to those around you, leading them to the heart of Christ.

Read the following verse to yourself in a low voice until you can say it with your eyes closed. This is the truest sense of meditation. Allow the word of God to dwell in you richly, bringing forth images and thoughts of God's unreasonable love.

> *For we are a fragrance of Christ to God among those who are being saved and among those who are perishing* (2 Cor. 2:15).

What kinds of words, thoughts or images came to mind as you meditated on the scripture? Describe them here.

What do these images and thoughts reveal to you about the heart of God? Write your comments here.

Now put yourself in the picture. What is the Lord saying to you personally through the scripture and the revelations you have received? Record your revelations here.

EXPERIENCE THE PRESENCE

Mercy is a fragrant love that will lead you back to the Father's heart. Just as with the honeysuckle, this fragrance is overwhelming in its sweetness. Nothing can surpass it. Allow this fragrance to fill your heart.

Put yourself in a place of quiet safety and close your eyes to allow yourself to be surrounded with this His fragrant love. You may place yourself in the images the Lord gave you as you meditated on the scripture or any other safe place where you can meet with Him. Breathe in His fragrant love for you and write down any further thoughts or images that you sense the Lord communicating to you.

SEE THE GLORY

Over the coming days take time to be in a quiet place if even for a few minutes and breathe in the Lord's fragrant love. Keep a journal of any times you sense an invitation into His fragrant presence. Also recall times when you have the opportunity to carry that fragrance to others who need it.

CHAPTER 2

Turned Toward Mercy

"THE CHERUBIM SHALL HAVE THEIR WINGS SPREAD UPWARD, COVERING THE MERCY SEAT WITH THEIR WINGS AND **FACING ONE ANOTHER**; THE FACES OF THE CHERUBIM ARE TO BE **TURNED TOWARD THE MERCY SEAT**" (EXOD. 25:20, EMPHASIS MINE).

KYLE'S STORY

How did I get myself into this place? Here I was, standing in a light drizzle between two sets of gray prison bars, all alone. What had I gotten myself into this time? I had ministered in county jails several times, but this was a larger, state facility where hard-core criminals were being held, hopefully under secure conditions. I should be safe, shouldn't I? I have to be honest and say that this was the last place I ever expected to learn about the mercy of God. I didn't associate mercy with my mental stereotype of unshaven inmates walking around in striped suites, bound with shackles and chains.

I found myself behind these prison bars through the help of some friends of our ministry who work as correctional officers in this state prison. During a ministry trip they had told me the story of a man they had come to know well in the prison, a man whose life had been converted and transformed by the power of God's mercy. I was so moved by their description of this man of God that I knew I just had to meet him, so I asked them to arrange such a meeting.

As I arrived at the prison, I entered the visitor's center where my name appeared on the clergy visitor's list. I had to be approved, however, before I would be able to sit with this man who was serving a long prison sentence for several crimes he had committed in his younger years. After they checked my name on the list, I was asked to surrender practically everything that identified who I was.

Though I had come to interview this man, I was told that I was not even allowed to take a legal pad or pen with me. In fact, I could take nothing. I was just hoping the Ginkgo root would kick in and allow my middle-aged brain to remember the important parts of our upcoming conversation! I was asked to remove all valuables and forms of identification and put them in a locker. Then I had to wait until my name and the name of the inmate were called.

I sat for a while and watched the families of prisoners who were coming in and sitting down around me. There were mothers, fathers, wives, and children, and they all looked pretty normal to me. I don't know what I really expected. After what seemed like a long time, my prisoner's name was called and I was guided to a metal detector where I had to take off my shoes and belt and pass through to the "no-man's land" on the other side. Then an officer pointed to a door and rattled off some rote and muddled directions to the building where such visits take place. He pointed to a door and told me that I would have to go the rest of the way *alone*.

I walked through the door and outside to a gate or "grill," as they called it. I walked in one side and heard the hum of an electric motor as the grill closed behind me, leaving me in a temporary cage. After a few seconds the grill on the opposite side of the cage opened with the same impersonal, not-in-a-hurry speed. I then walked through the drizzle to the doorway of the building where I would meet this man who had been described to me as being completely filled with the glory of God.

However, I was beginning to feel as though I had made a mistake. I looked at the weatherworn brick walls of the prison and asked myself, "Man, what in the world are you doing in this place?" I spoke to God and said something like this, "Well, here's another fine mess you've gotten me into!"

I walked through a succession of checkpoints with each grill clanking behind me and separating me from all that I knew and all that I was. It was as if I had said good-bye to freedom. My only identity now was a small, worn, green plastic-covered badge that was clipped to my shirt. All of my personal identity and freedom had been taken from me, and I was more than a little nervous.

Believe me, there were at least equal amounts of doubt and anointing within me as I walked through the stations of blank institutional personnel in their plain, dark-blue uniforms. All I had was me and the gentle nudging of what I hoped was the Spirit of God leading me to an encounter with my Father's heart.

At last I arrived at the top of the stairs where I was to meet this transformed man. Finally, I thought. Then I was taken into a room where I saw only two lines of cold metal folding chairs facing each other. I was not sure what to expect, but I knew what I was looking for, or at least I thought I did. From the stories I had been told by the men who had guarded this prisoner and held him in very high esteem, I had formed a picture in my mind of some grizzled old "lifer" who was dressed in prison denim blues. I assumed that the man would have tattoos and scars from prison riots and drug deals that had gone bad.

I had conjured up a picture in my mind, the product of hazy discernment and old prison movies, and I expected to see a weathered man with a kind, deeply lined face that revealed the story of the hard time he had served. But, as I entered the room, I was somewhat taken aback by the reality I beheld, for I was approached by a youthful person in his mid-thirties. He had blond hair and bright, receptive blue eyes. This young man looked like a computer engineer rather than a prison inmate.

Actually, Kyle looked no different than any yuppie guy you might expect to see at Starbucks reading the paper and sipping expensive coffee. He was not what I had envisioned as a man who was serving a more-than-thirty-year sentence in a secure facility after being convicted for armed robbery and attempted murder.

We shook hands and sat down, facing each other as we took our seats in cold, gray, metal chairs. There were others who were sitting on either side of us in this very public place where it seemed impossible to have a truly personal encounter or conversation.

As I sat in front of Kyle, I looked at him straight in the eye. What I saw greatly fascinated me. His face was radiant with the peace of God even though he resided in this very frightening place.

The man then introduced himself to me, and everything within me wanted to shout, "Kyle, what in God's name are you doing in this place?" After a few moments, however, my eyes grew accustomed to the light of God's glory that radiated from his face, and I simply asked Kyle to tell me his story.

He told me that he grew up in a fatherless home and was using drugs by the age of ten. He spent his teen years under the growing influence of many drugs, including his drug of choice, PCP, an acronym for Phencyclidine. His desire for PCP and other drugs controlled Kyle and dominated every aspect of his life even though he was looking for a place of rest and comfort in his out-of-control life.

By the age of seventeen, Kyle had turned his life completely over to crime and drugs. During one of the robberies he participated in, Kyle and his brother believed they had killed a man, so they threw his body into a river. The two young men were sure he was dead. So, thinking that they had committed a murder and, therefore, had nothing more to lose, they went on a spree of armed robberies. Amazingly, however, their victim did not die.

Eventually, Kyle and his brother were apprehended, and they were sent to a maximum-security prison. While in this prison, the two of them got on the wrong side of some other dangerous men because they had assaulted another prisoner. Many of the men who were incarcerated there were serving life sentences, and they felt they had nothing to lose by engaging in violent behavior. A group of six of these convicts was determined to find and kill Kyle because his brother had stabbed their friend.

Kyle got wind of their plan and prepared himself for battle by wielding a knife in each of his hands. But, as he was leaving his cell, Kyle's eyes took notice of a copy of *The Living Bible* his mother had just sent to him. His mother had been a constant and gentle presence in his life, and she had been praying that Kyle would turn to Jesus and find his place of safety and security in the midst of all the chaos and violence of prison life.

In that instant Kyle paused to pick up the green-covered book, and he uttered a prayer that he told me he didn't even mean. He prayed, "Lord, get me out of this place and I will put you first." That brief moment passed and Kyle put aside the Bible and forgot about the prayer as soon as it left his mouth.

Now, not knowing whether he would ever return, Kyle walked numbly out of his cell. Holding knives in both of his hands, he thought he was heading to his demise. He went to the lower level of a common area in the farthest corner to wait for the inevitable confrontation. He could hear the shuffling feet of the six men who were coming to get him. An older man who was sitting there and playing checkers with his friend calmly announced, "Here they come!"

Kyle saw his "execution party" walking slowly down the stairs. Surprisingly, time passed slowly, and it seemed to take them all day to walk down only one flight of stairs. Just to demonstrate how serious their murderous intentions toward Kyle were, one of the men turned and stabbed an innocent and otherwise uninvolved man who was sitting nearby! Kyle's heart was pounding in his ears as they approached, and he faced them with his back to the corner like a frightened rat that was ready to kill or be killed.

Suddenly, before the men could actually reach him, a riot involving guards and other inmates erupted because another man had just been killed! In the resulting confusion, the six men who had come to kill Kyle turned and simply walked in the other direction.

Prison guards then began to launch tear gas into the common area where the riot had broken out. In the chaos that followed, Kyle was taken out of the area and sent to a different super-maximum facility. The prison administration believed that he had been part of the riot that had injured several guards. Kyle had not really been involved with that melee, however.

When he arrived at the super-max lockup, Kyle was thrown roughly into a solitary cell and was stripped of everything, including his shoes. As he sat there, all alone, naked, and barefoot, he suddenly realized that the short and unintended prayer he had uttered in the previous facility had been answered! This realization caused a chill to race up his spine.

God's methods were not what Kyle had in mind when he said that prayer, but God *had* saved his life, and He had removed him from the threat of death by placing him in super-maximum security. Now his eyes, which still stung from the tear gas, began to fill with the first real tears he had shed in a long time.

In that moment Kyle felt as if he was being held in a warm embrace, and he suddenly remembered that he used to love Jesus. He felt the presence of God in that place of solitary confinement, and it was as real as anything he had ever experienced. It was a love as great and real as the fear he had experienced the previous day. This spiritual experience felt like his mother's embrace. It was the moment of Kyle's conversion to Christ.

From that moment on Kyle has wanted to embrace the God who embraced him. A few days after his conversion, the chaplain, whom Kyle had not yet met, sent him a *Living Bible* just like the one his mother had sent to him. It was just like the Bible he had gripped the day before, as he anticipated the battle he thought he would have to fight. You see, Kyle's Father in heaven had anticipated his hunger for His Word and His presence, and He tightened His loving embrace around His newly adopted son.

Though Kyle didn't become a choirboy overnight and he still had to go through many struggles, he began to grow in the mercy, grace, and knowledge of God. He read and studied the *Living Bible* that God had put in his hands and began to cultivate an awareness of the Lord's presence. As he was embraced in the heart of God, it became obvious to Kyle that his Father had been with him all along and had rescued and helped him many times throughout his life.

A shift was taking place in Kyle's heart and mind. The self-security that Kyle had created was being replaced by the embrace of the Father he had never known, the Father that had watched him and longed for a relationship with him every day of his life. Kyle began to understand the mercy of God that had been invested in him, and he reasoned, "If God could save someone like me, what kind of God must He be? If He loves me, He must love everyone." Kyle had begun to see himself as the Father saw him, and from that vantage point it was not a big leap to see others as the beloved children of God.

As the secure embrace of God's compassion grew stronger in his life, Kyle began to actually *see* the other, older inmates who were around him. Some of them had grown angry and embittered by their long lives in prison. They seemed to feel shut away and removed from the presence of God and any kind of love.

Over time Kyle began to speak to these older men, and he would read the Bible to them. He discovered that many of them were illiterate and could not read the Bible for themselves. As Kyle read the Word to them and encouraged them, he told them of the love of God and shared his own story with them. He felt that it was as if the Lord was speaking to him and through him as he spoke to the other prisoners.

This young man of God began to realize that he had always been carried in the embrace of the Father. Now, fully aware that he was safely in the Father's embrace, Kyle learned how to carry others. Like the Apostle Paul, Kyle had become the prisoner of Jesus Christ. (See Eph. 3:1.)

This prisoner of Christ began to visit older and terminally ill inmates. He would read to them and sometimes even hold their hands at the moments of their physical deaths. He would sometimes shave them or wash them, and in so doing he would bring them into the embrace of the Father's compassion and merciful love.

Kyle prayed for many years with one man who was dying from liver disease. As time wore on, the man became very thin and looked almost like a skeleton. The dying man put his bony arms around Kyle, rested his head against the hollow of his neck, and acknowledged the Father's embrace. With his final breaths, the dying man gave his heart to Christ. The fight for life was almost over, and his face was turned toward the Father's. Now safe in the Father's compassionate embrace, as the man began to pray for Kyle, he passed into the eternal embrace of His loving and merciful God.

Eventually, Kyle became part of the prison hospice, which was known as Prisoners Caring for Prisoners, or PCP, for short. This was a different kind of PCP than the drug he had surrendered to in his earlier days. Through the years Kyle has surrendered more and more of his life to the Lord, and all along he says that he has experienced the compassionate, loving, and merciful embrace of His heavenly Father.

The love of God turned Kyle away from his pain and toward the mercy of God, and this allowed him to see something greater than himself. He now sees the needs of the ones around him and cares for those who cannot care for themselves—those who seem to be "used up."

Kyle told me, "As I love them, I am loving Jesus." Then he quoted Matthew 25 to me in the words of *The Living Bible* that he now treasured: "When you did it to these my brothers you were doing it to me" (Matt. 25:40, LB).

A FURTHER CONVERSION

A further conversion awaits the children of God. What Kyle experienced was a true conversion that was evidenced by the fact that he became a different man—a man who grew to be more like Jesus. In other words, Kyle's life was *turned toward mercy*.

The word that is translated as "conversion" in the New Testament literally means to "turn toward."[1] In Kyle's conversion he was *turning toward* the heart of God—becoming what he had found in the heart of the Father who was embracing him.

The conversion that Kyle experienced results in a new way of life that leads to ultimate peace with God and man. It is a conversion that turns one away from self and allows one to "... always please the Lord and honor him, so that you will always be doing good, kind things for others, while all the time you are learning to know God better and better" (Col. 1:10, LB).

A picture of this new way of life is seen in the Torah, as God gave instructions to Moses regarding the dimensions for making the *mercy seat*—the seat of His earthly government.

> *You shall make two cherubim of gold, make them of **hammered work** at the two ends of the mercy seat. Make one cherub at one end and one cherub at the other end; you shall make the cherubim of **one piece with the mercy seat** at its two ends. The cherubim shall have their wings spread upward,*

*covering the mercy seat with their wings and **facing one another**; the faces of the cherubim are to be **turned toward the mercy seat...There I will meet with you**; and from above the mercy seat, from between the two cherubim which are upon the ark of the testimony, I will speak to you about all that I will give you in commandment for the sons of Israel* (Exod. 25:18-20, 22, NASB, emphasis mine).

The *mercy seat* was the expression of God's heart and government on the earth. Two cherubim made from "hammered work" stood at opposite ends of the mercy seat, facing each other. These representatives of God's heart and presence literally stand in mercy themselves. They were to be "one piece" with mercy, "turned toward" each other and also "turned toward the mercy seat" of God.

Beloved, we are in the place of those two cherubim. We too have been "hammered" in the sense that we have experienced hurts and wounds, but we've also experienced the restoring mercy of a loving Father. When we are turned toward the mercy of God, our wounds can actually become a source of compassion and understanding for the other wounded ones around us. You and I may bring the wounded and alienated to the mercy seat so as to allow the face of the Father to shine on them and heal them.

The Lord said that He would "meet" with, literally "word"[2] with, us at the mercy seat. The mercy seat communicates the mercy of God. It is in mercy that we see the heart of God—when we express love in mercy we express the heart of God. Kyle, the prisoner of Christ, began to see others through the eyes of mercy. God invited him to the mercy seat and then Kyle began to bring others there as well, as his heart was turning toward mercy and he himself was becoming a mercy seat.

As we look at the mercy seat, we see the emblems of God's heart and character. In the mercy seat God was bringing us closer to Him. Mercy is the very expression of His nature and His ultimate glory on earth. The Father was so serious and passionate about His love for us that He *revealed* His heart in the mercy seat to Moses, then *became* a mercy seat in Christ so that you and I might become a mercy seat for the nations. Mercy is the vehicle through which the heart of heaven comes to earth, filling it with His glory.

As we *turn toward mercy*, we are filled with the passion of God, and we express the presence of God by giving glory to God. These important three truths form the three sections of this book: Mercy, the *Passion*, the *Presence* and the *Glory* of God.

On a personal level, this immersion into the heart of the Father has healed and changed me. God, in His great mercy toward me, has allowed me to come to the mercy seat and accept His love, mercy, and grace. Consequently, I have learned that He loves me and wants me always to come near to Him.

In light of all this, I am writing a far different book than the one I first set out to compose. I have endeavored to respond to the gentle presence of God and present mercy as the expression of the Father's heart rather than as a theological proposition. Whenever we are in the presence of His heart, we are changed—converted—turned toward all that He is. It is my greatest aim to help us all to *turn toward mercy* and see the earth filled with the glory of God.

> The quality of mercy is not strained;
> It droppeth as the gentle rain from heaven
> Upon the place beneath.
> It is twice blest;
> It blesseth him that gives and him that takes.
> 'Tis mightiest in the mightiest; it becomes
> The throned monarch better than his crown.
> His sceptre shows the force of temporal power,
> The attribute to awe and majesty,
> Wherein doth sit the dread and fear of kings;
> But mercy is above this scept'red sway;
> It is enthroned in the hearts of kings;
> It is an attribute to God himself,
> And earthly power doth then show likest God's
> When mercy seasons justice. [3]

ENDNOTES

1 epistrepho (ep-ee-stref'-o); from NT:1909 and NT:4762; to revert (literally, figuratively or morally): KJV - come (go) again, convert, (re-) turn (about, again). (Biblesoft's New Exhaustive Strong's Numbers and Concordance with Expanded Greek-Hebrew Dictionary. Copyright (c) 1994, Biblesoft and International Bible Translators, Inc.)

2 From the Hebrew word *dabar,* which is a unit of communication.

3 William Shakespeare, *The Merchant of Venice* (Portia at IV, i).

Turning Points

FEEL THE PASSION

Dear one. The Father is inviting you to turn your eyes and your heart toward mercy—toward His face. Experience the passion of the Father's heart for you as you meditate on the scripture below. Read it aloud to yourself several times until you can close your eyes and speak it to yourself. Focus the eyes of your heart on the presence of God as you read this verse:

> *"Come to Me, all who are weary and heavy-laden, and I will give you rest"* (Matt. 11:28).

What kinds of pictures, images or thoughts come to mind as you meditate on this scripture? Write them here.

What do these images or thoughts reveal to you about the heart of God?

Now put yourself in the picture. What is the Lord speaking to your heart personally?

EXPERIENCE THE PRESENCE

In what areas does your heart need to be turned toward mercy for yourself? You will know the answer to this, because those areas are places of heaviness. They are places where you are trying to make it on your own or where you are trying to protect yourself, as Kyle did, with a weapon in each hand.

Picture yourself in a safe place with the presence of the Lord and then invite the Lord to reveal any area of heaviness in your life. This safe place may be the image or setting that came to mind while you meditated on the scripture above. The safe place may be one where you have met with Him regularly in the past or present.

Perhaps you are holding on to judgments or bitterness against someone who has wounded or disappointed you. There may be areas where you need to extend mercy to yourself. Now release these yokes and weights to the Lord and take His yoke of mercy upon yourself. List below any of these areas the Lord reveals to you which you release to Him.

SEE THE GLORY

Watch now for the Lord to move in your heart and life as you turn toward Him in confidence and give Him control in your life in the areas you mentioned above. Keep a journal about this, as you recognize areas in your life and heart that you need to surrender to Him where you can give the Lord glory for His mercy in your life.

CHAPTER 3

The Invitation

NOW THE LORD SAID TO MOSES, "COME UP TO ME ON THE MOUNTAIN AND REMAIN THERE, AND I WILL GIVE YOU THE STONE TABLETS WITH THE LAW AND THE COMMANDMENT WHICH I HAVE WRITTEN FOR THEIR INSTRUCTION." SO MOSES AROSE WITH JOSHUA HIS SERVANT, AND MOSES WENT UP TO THE MOUNTAIN OF GOD. THEN MOSES WENT UP TO THE MOUNTAIN, AND THE CLOUD COVERED THE MOUNTAIN. THE GLORY OF THE LORD RESTED ON MOUNT SINAI, AND THE CLOUD COVERED IT FOR SIX DAYS; AND ON THE SEVENTH DAY HE CALLED TO MOSES FROM THE MIDST OF THE CLOUD. AND TO THE EYES OF THE SONS OF ISRAEL THE APPEARANCE OF THE GLORY OF THE LORD WAS LIKE A CONSUMING FIRE ON THE MOUNTAIN TOP. MOSES ENTERED THE MIDST OF THE CLOUD AS HE WENT UP TO THE MOUNTAIN; AND MOSES WAS ON THE MOUNTAIN FORTY DAYS AND FORTY NIGHTS. (EXOD. 24:12-13, 15-18)

It was like fire. The presence of the invisible God settled on the top of the mountain in a thick cloud of glory that lit up with an unquenchable light. For six days and nights, this thick, pulsating inferno hovered over the mountain while the people stood in awe at a distance. To mere men, the glory of God looked like something that might consume them—something that would engulf and destroy them. This cloud remained over the summit of Sinai, drawing the attention of the people for six days and interrupting the darkness of six nights.

Now, on the seventh day, the Voice spoke from the middle of this thick and undulating brilliance: "Moses, come up to Me ..." The people below heard the invitation and looked to Moses, wondering what he might do. Surely he would not walk into the fire and certain destruction. Nevertheless, the Voice was clear and constant, "Moses, come up to Me."

Moses, now an ancient man, walked out of the doorway of his tent, and leaving everything behind, began to walk slowly up the side of the mountain navigating around dry and wind-worn desert rocks. The eyes of the people watched each labored step he took as he grew smaller in their sight and closer to the Voice that never ceased calling, "Moses, come ... come up to Me."

As Moses grew closer to the Voice, the air seemed to be alive and crackling with the Presence. The man who spoke to God face to face walked through the first wafting strains of cumulous glory and was taken from the eyes of the people at the bottom of the mountain. Moses simply disappeared into the glory of God. Now immersed in glory, Moses walked closer to the heart of the mist, walking through the fire and being consumed in the glory that surrounded him.

As Moses stood in the midst of the cloud, he was saturated with the essence of the Eternal Heart that enveloped him and clung to him like the dew of heaven. In that cloud, the heart of God was unveiled to Moses for forty days and nights, as he was surrounded and embraced in the presence and passion of the Ancient of Days. He was transformed within the very heart of God.

In the cloud of God's presence and glory, the stream of time emptied deeply into the sea of the eternal, and the end could be seen from the beginning. Peering through time in every direction, Moses saw the reality of the Father's heart being unfolded and manifested. In the distant future he could see that another cloud of glory would cover another mountain—the mount where the Son of God was transfigured and clothed in "garments ... radiant and exceedingly white, as no launderer on earth can whiten them" (Mark 9:3). And in that day Moses, the shadow, saw Christ, the Substance, each one consumed in the heart of the Father and longing for the other to be fulfilled. (See Heb. 10:1.)

In that fiery, pulsating mist, all that God was became translated into a physical representation of the Eternal Heart. As God took Moses from one aspect of His heart to the next, He disclosed a "pattern" from heaven that would represent His heart to men on earth. The Eternal spoke out of the deepest realm of His heart and told of His desire to settle among men in a way they could touch and be touched by Him. Moses was consumed in the intimate beating of the Father's heart for those forty days and nights. In the heart of that heart was the mercy seat.

Turning Points

FEEL THE PASSION

Meditate on this scriptural truth by speaking it aloud to yourself in a low tone until you can say with your eyes closed. As you meditate on this word, listen to the Father's invitation. He is calling you by name.

"I have called you by name; you are Mine!" (Isa. 43:1)

What images, thoughts or pictures come to your mind as the truth of the Father's love for your sinks into your heart through this scripture? Write them here.

What do these images or thoughts reveal to you about the heart of God? Now put yourself in the picture. What is the Lord speaking to you personally? Write it here.

EXPERIENCE THE PRESENCE

Beloved, the God who created and formed you is inviting you to enter into a new realm of intimate relationship with Him. He longs to have you know His heart for you—to heal you. Pause now and listen for the voice of the One who calls you to a more intimate fellowship with Him. Feel His personal presence as He says to you, *"You are mine."*

Experience the Father's personal presence as you enter the cloud as Moses did. Feel the moist, dewy cloud of His presence as you are embraced by the warmth of His love. Listen to the words He speaks over you and write them below. He may impress your heart with simple thoughts and words. Write them down here.

SEE THE GLORY

Over the coming days be aware of the Lord's personal presence around you. Take note of each time you sense His invitation for you to "come up" to Him. Allow your heart to be focused and settled as you live in the cloud of the Lord's glory.

CHAPTER 4

Called to be Consumed

God has invited us, "Come up to Me ..." to a more intimate place in Him. How many times have we heard His invitation in one form or another? It seems like a good idea to draw closer to God. But the Scriptures tell us that "our God is a consuming fire." (See Deut. 4:24 and Heb. 12:29.) If we respond to that invitation as Moses did, we, like him, will have to walk into the certain destruction and incineration of our flesh.

Who wants to be consumed? Not me. I don't know about you, but every waking minute my flesh is trying to stay alive and keep itself going. Now, when I'm talking about my flesh, I'm not merely referring to my physical body. I'm talking about my natural tendencies, my priorities, and my opinions, all of which want to "eat" too much and pray too little. My flesh wants to be coddled and it recoils at the thought of any kind of pain. Pain! Are you kidding?! If my flesh doesn't want to get up off the couch to take out the trash, there is a good chance that it doesn't give any thought to being consumed by anything, especially not love or concern for someone else's need.

My flesh only loves itself and it wants to consume, not to be consumed. I am more disposed to pizza than pity for you. "I know I am rotten through and through so far as my old sinful nature [flesh] is concerned" (Rom. 7:18, LB). My flesh is nobody's entree, but there are issues and thoughts that eat at me, and there are some places in my heart that are not very well hidden, places where my flesh wants to triumph and do an "end-zone dance" all over someone's head when he or she wrongs or threatens me.

Not long ago I was in a meeting with some Christian brothers, and I was astonished to hear some of them sharing a point that I had tried to make in a previous meeting. When I had shared that same point before, they had responded by discounting and rebuffing me! However, they had somehow suddenly come to the very same conclusion that had caused a sense of separation of hearts during the earlier meeting. Everything inside of me wanted to jump up and shout, "You dummies! I said the same thing before and some of you blew me off and looked at me like I was crazy!" Now, wouldn't that have been a merciful and mature response on my part?

I must admit that I'm not very good at disappearing into fiery clouds like Moses did. I want to be seen and appreciated, and I want to be *right*! I want to draw only enough attention to myself and my needs to let everyone know how humble and selfless I am. I want the bigger half of the candy bar, and I am willing to point out to the world when I get the smaller piece. In other words, I want my "pound of flesh." When someone offends me, my flesh wants to "jump out of its seat" and defend itself.

Mercy, however, is a fiery, consuming love that is opposed to the interests of my flesh. Many times we are content to be warmed by lesser fires: the fires of anger, unforgiveness, pride, judgments, and religion, which all become wood on more friendly and comforting fires. My soul wants to lie *in front* of the fire like an old hound dog, not to disappear into it. All of these lesser fires seem safer than God's invitation to enter and experience His consuming love.

In his novel *Les Miserables*, Victor Hugo provides a picture of the consuming love of God. One man, Jean Valjean, was shown a single act of mercy that transformed and redeemed his life. He was caught red-handed with stolen goods that would have landed him in prison at hard labor for the rest of his life. In fact, he was guilty, and he deserved punishment. Valjean, a rough and hardened criminal, had stolen table silver from a compassionate priest. Valjean was caught with the silver by the local gendarme and taken back to the priest, whereupon the kindly cleric scolded him for not taking the silver candlesticks that completed the set.

Astonished, the police had to release Valjean to the mercy of the priest who held his life in his hands. The priest spoke to him, "Jean Valjean, my brother, you no longer belong to evil, but to good. It is your soul that I am buying for you. I withdraw it back from dark thoughts and from the spirit of perdition, and I give it to God."[1] This single act of kindness grew throughout Valjean's life, bearing fruit in the lives of many around him Valjean was consumed by the love of God.

On the other hand, there was Inspector Javert, who pursued Valjean for many years to bring him back to prison. In the end, the tables were turned during a time of the French revolution. Valjean had Javert's life in his hands, but he spared him and then turned himself over to Javert and the law that had pursued him those many years. Javert, now face to face with the insurmountable, irrational power of mercy, released Valjean and threw himself into the river. The consuming love of God had come near Valjean and *mercy had triumphed over justice*. (See James 2:13.) Jean Valjean walked in the light of that silver candlestick all the rest of his life and *became* what was shown to him: mercy.[2]

The difference in the response of Javert and the priest who extended the consuming love of God is found in what they *saw*. Javert saw only an infraction of law while the priest saw the hungry Valjean. One saw the *deed* and the other the *need*. Mere justice was consumed in love. Mercy cost the priest the physical pain of assault at the hands of Valjean and it also cost him his personal treasure. The priest saw the heart of the man and redeemed him with silver. Mercy saw the need and chose to love.

In our ministry I sit with couples who are blind to one another. They see only the offenses against them and are focused on their own pain. A woman, let's call her Kate, came to me once with the complaint that her husband was not the spiritual head of their home. This precious and worn-out sister tearfully told me of her husband's isolation and his lack of desire to communicate with her. She was at the end of the road with him and ready to "throw in the towel" with regard to their marriage.

As I prayed with Kate I asked her to close her eyes and see her husband with the eyes of her heart. When Kate closed her eyes, she began to catch an image of her husband as a man behind a wall. I simply asked her, "Kate, why would any man hide behind a wall?"

She replied, "It's because he is not feeling safe." I simply prayed, "Lord, would you allow Kate to see her husband as you see him? Why does he not feel safe?" Kate caught a vision of her husband as a little boy growing up in isolation and fear. She saw that her tactic of labeling her husband as a spiritual weakling actually caused him to retreat behind a wall of self-protection. As she saw the reality of her husband's heart, her flesh was consumed with compassion and she was able to respond to his fear instead of continuing to react out of her flesh. The result was healing for two hearts.

Beloved, something will consume us—it will be either the love of God or the love of self. We will bring glory either to our pain or our passion for the face of God. The scripture tells us, "Precious in the sight of the Lord is the death of His saints." (Psalm 116:15 NKJV). The death that is precious to God, in all likelihood, is the death of self. Yet many times we chose to remain far away from the very One whose breath we carry, the One who longs to love us.

LIVING AT A DISTANCE

When God speaks to us, He can only speak from His nature, and His very nature *is* mercy! We, like the people of ancient Israel, hear God, but we do not come close to Him. If they had chosen to get near to Him, their flesh would have been consumed. We see this truth revealed in the words of the Israelites after the Lord gave them the Law:

> ...'Behold, the LORD our God has shown us His glory and His greatness, and we have heard His voice from the midst of the fire; we have seen today that God speaks with man, yet he lives. Now then why should we die? For this great fire will consume us; **if we hear the voice of the LORD our God any longer, then we will die**" (Deut. 5:24-25).

Sin and self-centeredness cause God's beloved to remain at a distance from Him. When we hear the voice and heart of God, our flesh dies. For example, if someone offends us and God says, "Forgive them," our flesh will have to be consumed in order to obey God. If we hold some kind of judgment against another, and God tells us to see their heart and release them, our flesh will be consumed. Whenever we have to go to the back of the line, our flesh is consumed.

When someone struggles, we will do what seems "reasonable" and "right," but we will very seldom do what is needed. When we are consumed by mercy, "It is no longer I who live, but Christ lives in me" (Gal. 2:20), and we are then "... hidden with Christ in God" (Col. 3:3).

God is not content to have us stay at a safe distance from Him. He calls us to Himself and will not rest until we leave our place of safe religion and disappear into His heart. God called Moses to Himself on the seventh day—not to a place of temporary visitation, but to a place of rest.

We love the safe, comforting fire of religion with all of its predictable patterns and programs. People love the forms of religion, because these forms really don't require them to change; instead, they merely adapt. Such adherence to the forms of religion does not lead to transformation, which must take place in the heart. Without heart transformation, we tend to worship the pattern at the expense of intimacy with the person of God. David had it right when He got rid of the extraneous furnishings of religion and brought the presence of God to Zion, where he could live with and rule in and from God's presence (2 Sam 6:17).

The greatest thing that is consumed by mercy is the distance between hearts. Jesus, the express image of the Father, was consumed by the glory of the Father as well. The thing that was consuming Jesus was the dwelling place of God among men. Jesus allowed Himself to be completely consumed by the love of God so as to make such a close and open relationship possible.

The Gospel of John applies a prophetic scripture to Jesus by saying, "His disciples remembered that it was written, 'ZEAL FOR YOUR HOUSE WILL CONSUME ME'" (John 2:17). What was it that was eating at Jesus? Was He crazy for a house or a religious

structure? No! He was not concerned with stones and carpets, but He was focused on the household, the *oikos* of God. Jesus was eaten up by the dwelling place of God, the same thing that consumed the heart of the Father. It was His desire to be with us that allowed the whip of cords to be placed in the hands of those who murdered the Son of God. Jesus was consumed by the love of the Father. One Psalm that Jesus' disciples remembered reads, "For zeal for Your house has consumed me, And the reproaches of those who reproach You have fallen on me" (Ps. 69:9).

CONSUMED FOR HIS GLORY

Any time our flesh is consumed, the Shekinah[3] of God's very presence forms, and the glory rebounds to God. When Solomon dedicated the Temple of God on Mt. Zion, a sacrifice of flesh was placed upon the altar. When the prayer of dedication was concluded, fire fell from heaven and consumed the offering. Then the scriptures say, "Fire came down from heaven and consumed the burnt offering and the sacrifices, and the glory of the LORD filled the house" (2 Chron. 7:1). That cloud of glory was the smoke of incinerated flesh. The principle is clear: if flesh is presented to God, He will consume it and the house will be filled with the glory of God. When the glory of God was manifested, the priests began to sing, "For He is good, For His mercy endures forever" (2 Chron. 7:3, NKJV). Mercy *is* the glory of God!

Beloved, we are called into the Father's heart, and in His heart there is an unquenchable love—a consuming love that will destroy all flesh that is presented to it. We are called to be consumed with whatever consumes the heart of God. In the process of this consuming, our flesh becomes fuel for His glory.

I remember once being in a barbershop when an old man walked in. He was well dressed in a plaid sport jacket, and he was wearing a tie. His dress and appearance provided a noticeable contrast to the others who were seated in chairs, waiting for their turn in a barber's chair. The old gentleman was somewhat frail and soft-spoken. He looked as if he was in his eighties, and it was obvious that he was a bit confused about where he was—perhaps he was in the early stage of some form of dementia. It soon became clear to me that he would be a little stretched if he had to wait in a chair for his turn.

I knew my turn was coming up next, and I thought it would be good to let this gent take my turn. I realized, however, that if that were to happen, it would affect everybody else who was in line behind me. It was a decision, therefore, that needed to be made in consultation with the other two men who were rightfully in line ahead of this older gentleman. In light of all this, I quietly asked the others if it would be okay to give this man a break. They graciously agreed with my suggestion without any hesitation. In the end, the man was able to get into the chair in a few minutes, and he never realized that we had shown him mercy. We did so for one reason: simply because he needed it. This getting to the back of the line sent up a sweet savor into the nostrils of God. The old barbershop had become like the Holy of Holies, and the very heart of God was revealed by a simple act of mercy.

ENDNOTES

1 Victor Hugo, *Les Miserables* (New York: Simon & Schuster, Inc., 1964).
2 Note that Valjean's name seems to reflect the Hebrew name that comes from the root for *grace* and that Javert's name reflects the Latin word for *truth* or *justice*.
3 From the word *shakkan*, to dwell as in a cloud.

Turning Points

FEEL THE PASSION

Just as God called Moses into His consuming glory cloud, He now calls you. Quiet your heart and allow the fiery cloud of God's glory to settle over you. Meditate on the following scripture by speaking it aloud to yourself in a low tone until you can say it with your eyes closed. Let its truth wash over you.

> *Then the LORD God called [insert your name here] and said, "Where are you?"* (Gen. 3:9)

What kinds of pictures, images or thoughts come to mind as you meditated on this text? Write them down here. These are personal words the Lord has spoken to you, as you respond to His invitation.

What do these thoughts or images reveal to you about the heart of God?

Now put yourself in the picture. What is the Lord speaking to you personally? Write his words to you here.

EXPERIENCE THE PRESENCE

Quiet your heart now and picture yourself in a safe place with the Lord. You may be able to step into one of the images you received as you meditated on the scripture above. Let everything else fade away as you watch and listen for the Lord in stillness as you consider the fiery cloud of His presence. Allow the Lord to reveal anything to you that has distracted you from His presence and purpose for you.

Where have you been keeping yourself at a safe distance from God? List anything that comes to mind and then present these things to the Lord's fiery presence to be consumed.

SEEING THE GLORY

In the coming days be aware of areas of carnality the Lord brings to your attention, everything that distracts your attention, and write them down here. These may be things or possessions you value more than intimacy with God. Then allow the Lord to consume those things that rob you of quietness and rest and rob the Lord of glory.

CHAPTER 5

The Mercy Seat

"YOU SHALL MAKE A MERCY SEAT OF PURE GOLD,
TWO AND A HALF CUBITS LONG AND ONE AND
A HALF CUBITS WIDE" (EXOD. 25:17).

While Moses was immersed in the heart of God for those forty days and nights the Lord revealed a physical pattern to represent the reality of His heart. The first thing God instructed Moses to make was an ark and atop that ark a *mercy seat*—a place where the Eternal could pitch His tent among the temporal. The mercy seat enthroned the passion of the Father who made Himself vulnerable to a chosen but bankrupt people who had no hope of finding their way back to the presence of God on their own.

The mercy seat was inspired by the needs of both God and man. Is it shocking to think that God needs mercy as much as we do? He does. God desires a relationship with us that is both personal and passionate. He is not content to leave us saved but separate. His passionate nature bids Him to bring us close to His heart. Mercy and the mercy seat represent a bold and scandalous move on God's part to make a way for us, the fallen, to relate to the Father. Mercy and the mercy seat send a clear and unambiguous statement to us that God wants us.

Mercy and the mercy seat represent the *passion* of God, the *presence* of God, and the very *glory* of God. Its various emblems and facets reveal deep truths that invite us to come close to God with confidence and boldness "…so that we may receive mercy and find grace to help in time of need" (Heb. 4:16).

As we look at mercy, we look not at an abstract theological concept or doctrine but at the very heart and character of God. Mercy is the key word that God uses to describe Himself.

So then, what *is* mercy?

THE MERCY OF GOD

Though this whole book is written to describe mercy as the heart and character of God, it might be helpful to have a simple and basic definition of mercy. *Mercy is the passionate love of the Father's heart meeting the desperate need of man. Love* and *need* are the key words in this definition.

I must confess that I am only growing in my understanding of the mercy of God. I used to think and act as though mercy was something I had to do rather than something I had to become. I understand the heart of God and its abundant lovingkindness better as I have become a grandfather than I ever did as a father or a child. I find, and those around me will tell you, that I cry more easily than ever before. Not because of sadness but because I have become a better "seer" of people's desperate needs.

The other day two of my grandchildren were in our home and one of them, as children are apt to do, fell down and bumped her head. Her sudden shock at feeling pain caused her to screw up her little face and extend her lower lip as tears began to flow. There is only one *automatic* and appropriate response to this distended quivering lower lip and that is to pick her up and kiss her and hug her and check out where the "boo boo" might be. (There was no boo boo, by the way, but she still got the love.) That response was one of mercy flowing toward the need.

God, of course, is far more than an earthly grandfather. He is the Creator of all, and He is thoroughly holy. Holiness is the nature of

God, but mercy is the very heart of God. It is not something He has to think about and to decide whether or not He will be merciful. He is mercy! He feels it every time we fall. He is not a crabby grandfather who stays at a distance when we turn away. He comes to get us—to turn our faces back to His. He picks us up each time we bump our heads. We cannot change the nature of God any more than we can change the time of day, though we can refuse His mercy as we operate in our own pride.

Mercy originates in God as part of His eternal character. "If we could remember that the divine mercy is not a temporary mood but an attribute of God's eternal being, we would no longer fear that it would someday cease to be. Mercy never began to be, but from eternity was; so it will never cease to be." [1]

The mercy of God and the mercy of man both have the same source: the heart and character of God. When we *show* mercy it is not of our own nature but the outbreaking of the Eternal Heart through us. "Compassion has no place in the natural order of the world which operates on the basis of necessity. Compassion opposes this order and is therefore best thought of as being in some way supernatural."[2] The world is not much inclined toward mercy. Dallas Willard relates his experience of mercy from his personal life:

"The worldly wise will, of course, say, 'Woe to the merciful, for they shall be taken advantage of.' And outside Heaven's rule there is nothing more true. My mother and father were bankrupt and lost their clothing business in the early 1930s before I was born. Those were the depression years and they simply could not make people pay for what they needed. Clothing was given 'on credit' when it was clear there would be no payment."

God has extended relationship to us who are bankrupt and have no way to repay the debt. Unlike the owners of the clothing business, the Father is boundless and will never run out of mercy—never run out of love with which to clothe us. Mercy flows from the very heart and character of God; it is the divine instinct. "*God is love*" (1 John 4:8). Note that God instructed Moses to make the mercy seat of "pure gold." Mercy issues from an incorruptible heart whose nature is love. Mercy is not part of our carnal nature, which spends itself trying to find pleasure. If we do love or have mercy there is usually something in it for us. Mercy is much higher and beyond us. "For as high as the heavens are above the earth, so great is His lovingkindness [mercy] toward those who fear [tremble in awe of] Him" (Ps 103:11). God is full of mercy—rich in mercy! Mercy pours like tears from the eyes of the Father who is moved by our need.

The mercy of God flows out of the love of God; it is the active, kinetic expression of love that flows toward our need much as electricity flows to a darkened lightbulb. Without the mercy of God we are in the darkness—hopelessly lost.

Love precedes *mercy*—and flows out of it as it says so many times throughout the Bible.

> *Remember me for this also, O my God, and **show mercy to me according to your great love*** (Neh. 13:22 NIV, emphasis mine).

> ***Have mercy** on me, O God, **according to your unfailing love*** (Ps. 51:1 NIV, emphasis mine).

> *But **because of his great love for us, God, who is rich in mercy, made us alive** with Christ even when we were dead in transgressions—it is by grace you have been saved* (Eph. 2:4-5 NIV, emphasis mine).

Again, mercy is *love* flowing toward *need*. When the heart of the Father hears the cries of His own children He moves in mercy to pick them up much like a father or mother would pick up a crying child. It is the need of the child that touches and alarms the instinct of the parent. The Father does not launch into a theological or philosophical debate as to the worthiness of the child; He just begins to flow toward the need, though sometimes the child may refuse His expression of love.

Throughout the Bible, God displays His love through mercy toward those in some kind of need. God is "A father of the fatherless and a judge for the widows is God in His holy habitation. God makes a home for the lonely; He leads out the prisoners into prosperity, Only the rebellious dwell in a parched land." (Ps 68:5-6). (See also

Hosea 14:3.) All of these are in places of helplessness—those who live beyond their own power. God allows His love to flow toward the poor. (See Dan. 4:27.)

Mercy is the fragrant embrace of God's love that overwhelms the need of the world and overcomes obstacles that separate hearts. It is the only hope for all kinds of relationships, whether God-to-man or man-to-man. Mercy is the glue that keeps our love honest toward each other. Love is not really love and, indeed, it cannot exist unless it is guaranteed by mercy.

Mercy acts in love despite all hurts or offenses; it gives beyond hurt, just as Dallas Willard's parents did, and it expects no repayment. When we extend mercy we are making the decision to become weak—to become vulnerable to the needy. Paul tells us that he himself became "weak to the weak" to win them to Christ. "To the weak I became weak, that I might win the weak; I have become all things to all men, so that I may by all means save some (1 Cor. 9:22). God's love for the weak and needy was stronger than their offense toward him.

God issued the pattern for the mercy seat because we needed it. In mercy we are given access to the eternal passion of a Father's heart. In the Torah, God *revealed* a mercy seat. In the New Covenant God *became* a mercy seat in Christ. God has invited us to come close for His own sake. He declares, "I, even I, am the one who wipes out your transgressions for My own sake …" (Isa. 43:25). God longs to reveal His heart to us so that He may build that same mercy seat in us through which the world will turn toward Him and make His praise glorious.

ENDNOTES

1 A.W. Tozer, *The Knowledge of the Holy* (New York: Harper & Row Publishers, 1961), 97.

2 John Berger (*Guardian*, Dec. 19, 1991), *The Columbia Dictionary of Quotations* (New York: Columbia University Press, 1998).

Turning Points

FEEL THE PASSION

Beloved, the Father has always loved you even at your worst, even when you struggle. He is inviting you to Himself and now draws you with mercy. Meditate on the following verse of scripture by saying it aloud to yourself in a low tone and repeating it until you can say it with your eyes closed.

> *"I have loved you with an everlasting love; Therefore I have drawn you with lovingkindness"* (Jer. 31:3).

What images, thoughts, or pictures occurred to you as you repeated these words to yourself? Be sure to write them down.

What do these images reveal about the heart of God?

Enter into this picture now. What is the Lord speaking to you personally? Write it here.

EXPERIENCE THE PRESENCE

Beloved, the Father has always loved you even at your worst, even when you struggle now. He is inviting you to Himself and now draws you with mercy. All of us have other issues or values that draw us— that have a gravitational pull on us. What pulls at your heart? Perhaps it is a failure or weakness that you cannot change. Perhaps it's a hurt or disappointment from the past or fear of the future. The Lord who is enthroned upon the mercy seat is inviting you to release everything that pulls at your heart to Him.

Now put yourself in a safe place in the presence of the Lord and ask Him to reveal everything that pulls on your heart and draws attention away from Him. Write a list here of anything the Lord brings to mind. Allow Him to draw you with the gravitational pull of His love for you.

SEEING THE GLORY

Keep a journal in the coming days of places, events or relationships in which you are aware that the Lord is drawing you to focus on His intimate presence. These are times when He wants to impart something new and personal to you. Go aside to be with Him. Write about those times of drawing and invitation here.

PART TWO

Mercy

THE PRESENT LOVE OF GOD

CHAPTER 6

An Intimate Love

THEN THE LORD GOD FORMED MAN OF DUST FROM THE
GROUND, AND BREATHED INTO HIS NOSTRILS THE BREATH OF LIFE;
AND MAN BECAME A LIVING BEING (GEN. 2:7).

It was about the middle of the sixth day when the Creator stepped
out of eternity and into the garden. He had created life everywhere,
including seas teaming with fish and the air where birds seemed to
defy the newly written laws of gravity while the ink was still wet.
With every turn of the page, God created something more amazing
than the last, building excitement in creation itself at what He might
do next. All that He made was "good," but there was no one to share
it with Him—no living heart to return a thought or a word. There
was a longing for connection in the heart of God.

With His heart filled with love, the Eternal God walked over to a
little dry, dusty spot in the midst of paradise. Seeing something more
than dust, the Eternal put His hand into the red, dry, discorporate
particles and scooped some into His palms. Then, forming a cup with
his hands, God-in-the-flesh pulled His hands toward His mouth. Now
the Eternal began to exhale—to breathe onto the dust in His own
hands. "Hahhhhhhhh…" As He exhaled slowly, the condensation
of His breath moistened the dry dust. Then the Eternal gently pressed

His hands together, causing the moisture of His own eternal breath and the red dust of Eden to bond together into something moldable. He worked the moistened clay, passing it back and forth from one hand to the other, applying gentle pressure until it formed something that resembled His own form. The Eternal stepped back and looked at what He had created: *us*!

When He had completed His masterpiece, the Eternal spoke to us and said, "You are beautiful." We were not mere life like the other animals; we were alive! We looked back at the Eternal and caught His eye. Then, wonder of wonders, we spoke back to the One who molded us in His own hands what He longed to hear, "So are You."

WE TOOK HIS BREATH AWAY

We need more than a definition of mercy if we are to enter into the heart of God and turn our hearts toward mercy. From the moment *we* drew *His* first breath, the Eternal could not take His eyes off of us. We took His breath away! Beloved, God is a personal God who created us in His own eternal breath for the most intimate communion with Him. Imagine this: the very first conscious awareness of Adam was of being kissed alive by the Creator. We are the Artist's rendition of Himself—His handprints were still fresh on us. He knew every contour of our form and every thought in our hearts. Can you envision with me that when Adam met with God in the cool of the day (see Gen. 3:8), the very breath of God who formed him welled up in him and was exhaled back to Him in praise; "Hhhhhhaallelujah." Praise was our native tongue—our exhalation for His exaltation. We were created "… from Him and through Him and to Him" (Rom. 11:36).

God created us for connection with Him. He said, "I will also walk among you and be your God, and you shall be My people" (Lev. 26:12). Near the end of the New Testament, John the Beloved expresses the fruition of the Eternal's desire for us by saying, "Look, God's home is now among his people! He will live with them, and they will be his people. God himself will be with them" (Rev. 21:3-4, NLT). In every page of the Bible and in each beat of the Eternal Heart is the desire of God to be among men.

God is like other loving fathers who want to be with their children. I can't think of anything that grabs my heart more than the faces of my kids and grandkids. Our children look like us and remind us that there is something more to us than meets the eye—something eternal that will go on after we are returned to dust.

Before the foundation of the world, God has wanted us to live in His intimate presence—in love. (See Eph 1:4.) He is love. He is not only love, but He is also completely holy and righteous—totally flawless. "… God is Light, and in Him there is no darkness at all" (1 John 1:5). There is no darkness in God—no kind of shadowy doubt or variation. (See James 1:17.) We cannot say the same of man, however.

When we (in Adam) chose to believe the lie that we could live for ourselves and make it on our own, we forgot the warmth of eternal breath that held our dusty selves together and placed ourselves in the outer, breathless chill. Without that connection—without the breath of God—we are no more than dust. "If it were his intention and he withdrew his spirit and breath, all mankind would perish together and man would return to the dust" (Job 34:14-15, NIV).

Despite our turning our backs on God, He never changed His mind or desire for intimate relationship with us. But He could not become less than He was and still be God. This creates a serious dilemma in our relationship with God. How could a holy God be in the company of an unholy and rebellious people? How could the Incorruptible dwell among the corrupt? We are powerless to change our position before God one inch. We are stuck. But the Eternal is not.

Before He put His hand in the red dust of Eden to form man, God had made the decision that whatever it took; He was going to be in fellowship with us. He was prepared to step down out of time and eternity and become a lamb for the slaughter before He even invented lambs (see Rev. 13:8) in order to maintain the connection—all because He loves us. He can't help Himself: He *is* love! (See 1 John 4:8, 16.) *Love* moved out of the heart of God to draw us back to Him and became *mercy*.

It was mercy that allowed us to come back to God. Mercy is the intimate love of the Father's heart, or perhaps the love that leads us back to intimacy with Him. We have no way to make it back to God on our own. Mercy slew the animal with which God made a covering to hide our naked rebellion. Mercy guarantees love and keeps relationships together. Mercy is the love of His intimate intention toward us.

FACE-TO-FACE

Beloved, we were created Face-to-face to live face-to-Face with God. How else could God breathe His life into us but by being Face-to-face with us? My nostrils are on my face. How about yours? The only way God could have breathed into man's nostrils was by being Face-to-face with him, literally kissing man alive with His own breath!

In mercy, which is part of God's very nature (see Exod. 34:6), God remembers that He kissed us alive with His own breath. Is it a bit "squishy" for us to think of this? In his book *Secure in God's Embrace: Living As the Father's Adopted Child*, author Ken Fong speaks of two great kisses we receive—one kiss from the Father and one from the Son. Fong says, "The first great kiss is the initial kiss none of us can possibly remember, when the awesome God of the universe initializes the brain of every single human being with the sacred breath of life. The second great kiss is when Jesus, God's only Son, fills the heart of every new believer with the breath of new life through the Holy Spirit of God."

God makes the first move toward us in mercy. It's a kind of romantic love, really. He knows the dark towers of sin and separation we are locked up in and sets out to rescue us. He is willing to get His hands dirty, as He did at first when He picked up that dust and breathed into it. In mercy God came to rescue us from ourselves. The same breathy love that created us is the very thing that would allows us to be with Him.

God's relentless passion is for our presence—to see our faces. God is so passionate about seeing our faces that His first instruction in the Ten Commandments was that there would be nothing between our face and His. He literally said, "You shall have no other gods before my face" (Exod. 20:3).

His mercy allows us to be brought back to His face again. We were created Face- to-face to live face-to-Face. God is passionate about seeing our faces[1]—our presence.

There is a veritable no-man's land between our face and God's, and it is littered with the debris of moral failure and broken trust. What are we to do with all the offenses that leave the weight of judgments both from and against us?

Mercy breathes life into dead relationships, clearing away the junk between faces, whether of God or man. This passionate and breathy love of God breathes life wherever it is felt. When we are separated by sin or rebellion, God remembers His breath in us. Mercy brings life out of dust.

MERCY CREATES LIFE

The mercy of God is *a creative force that brings life and warmth wherever it is felt.* Mercy breathes life into the dead: dead hearts, dead relationships, dead works, and dead hopes.

Think about the heaps of dry bones the God of Abraham showed the prophet Ezekiel:

> *Then He (God) said to me, "**Prophesy to the breath**, prophesy, son of man, and say to the breath, 'Thus says the Lord GOD, "Come from the four winds, O breath, and breathe on these slain, that they come to life.""" So I prophesied as He commanded me, and the breath came into them, and they came to life and stood on their feet, an exceedingly great army* (Ezek. 37:9-10, emphasis mine).

When God was telling Ezekiel to prophesy to the breath, He was saying in effect, "Breathe on these dead and dusty bones." Here was a nation hopelessly separated and lying in the dust of their rebellion with nothing to reanimate them. God filled the prophet Ezekiel with His breathy love as he looked at heaps of dry and hopeless bones. The Lord breathed into dry bones and made them alive again.

We see the bony drought of relationships every day in our healing prayer ministry. I sat one evening with a couple—let's call them Jack and Jill. They had tumbled down to the bottom of the hill both with empty and dry pails. They sat across from each other shouting and weeping, each one dry and deafened inside by hurt. The pain and betrayal of adultery was living between their faces. They were caught in the bramble of their own hurts and were unable to *see* each other. Their marriage was like someone who was out of gas and trying to push the weight of a car down the road. They were exhausted and the breath had gone out of them.

As we prayed together, I asked each one to watch and listen to the other, and they were led, in turn, to the sources of their conflicts and pain through memory healing. First, we prayed with the husband and then with the wife, allowing the Lord to invite them to places of wounding. An amazing thing happened. Once they could peek around the pile of offenses and hurts that separated them, they discovered two wounded children locked up in lies and pain from the past. As each saw the other for perhaps the first time, the breath of God began to warm them, as compassion for the wounded children within them thawed the frozen wilderness between them. Their relationship and vision were changed forever. Now they are able to *respond* to one another in compassion instead of *reacting* out of their own pain. Mercy is miraculous! *It is alive!*

Mercy is like warm breath on hands that have been exposed to extreme cold. When we come in from the cold, we exhale onto our hands and rub them together until the feeling comes back. That's what mercy does: it exhales the love of God onto the frozen heart, allowing the feelings to return.

Mercy, the breathy love of God, allows us to see beyond the offense to the heart of the one who offended us and to bring them close to us again.

MERCY REVIVES

I can remember having the breath knocked out of me when I was a boy—that gasping sense of not having any breath and being unable to even draw in air if I could. A helpless paralysis took place whenever that happened. Sometimes I find myself flattened in the spirit as well— unable to draw breath—paralyzed and helpless.

When Jesus was crucified, the breath was knocked out of His disciples—they were flattened by His murder and they hid. When Jesus was resurrected, He could hardly wait to get to His deflated disciples. The first thing He did was to breathe the lost breath back into them again.

> *So when it was evening on that day, the first day of the week, and when the doors were shut where the disciples were, for fear of the Jews, Jesus came and stood in their midst and said to them, "Peace be with you." And when He had said this, He showed them both His hands and His side. The disciples then rejoiced when they saw the Lord. So Jesus said to them again, "Peace be with you; as the Father has sent Me, I also send you." And when He had said this,* **He breathed on them and said to them, "Receive the Holy Spirit** (John 20:19-22, emphasis mine).

Amazing! Jesus, God-in-the-flesh, breathed life into man again. The same breath that created man was breathed into him again to reestablish intimate connection through the blood and breath of Christ. This was the second kiss that Ken Fong talked about. God's mercy is the "artificial respiration" that breathes life back into the lost and calls them back into His presence.

MERCY CHANGES OUR FOCUS

Our self-focused nature distracts us from the face or presence of God. We tend to be fascinated with ourselves, and we're often focusing on what's wrong with us. Without the breathy love of God, we take our lives and the lives of others into our own hands. When someone hurts us, we gather up the evidence, form a posse, and get a rope. Why? It's because we can't *see* them, because we are focused on ourselves and on our pain, and we are numb to the heart of God. We are unaware of the eternal breath and hands that formed us.

Beloved, there is a refocusing that takes place through mercy. We are so used to "making it on our own," though we really cannot do so. If we are to be reconnected with the heart of God, we must come face-to-Face with Him and allow the Eternal to breathe His breath into us once again to overwhelm our dryness of heart. We must look at Jesus, the Father's fullest display of His intimate love and mercy.

Jesus, the greatest expression of the Father's heart, carries the breathy love of God to us, reviving us and redirecting our focus from ourselves to the face of God. We can trust the eternal breath in us to bring us close. He is, as Tennyson said, "Closer … than a breath and nearer than hands and feet."

ENDNOTES

1 The Hebrew word *paniym* is translated "face" or "presence."

Turning Points

FEEL THE PASSION

Now, focus on the presence of God as He walks through your heart, and allow Him to point out hurts and dry places—places where you need His intimate love for yourself or someone who has hurt you. Let Him breathe on those places. Focus on His presence by meditating on the Word below. Read it to yourself until you can close you eyes and see the scripture with the eyes of your heart:

> O God, You are my God; I shall seek You earnestly; My soul thirsts for You, my flesh yearns for You, In a dry and weary land where there is no water (Ps. 63:1).

What is the Lord saying to you? What kinds of images or thoughts came to you as you meditated on the scripture that has been breathed by God for you?

What do the images or thoughts that came to your mind reveal to you about the heart of God? Write it here.

Put yourself in the picture or thought now. What is the Lord speaking to you personally through His word and the images you have received? Write what you sense Him speaking to you here.

EXPERIENCE THE PRESENCE

Beloved, there are places where we have had the breath knocked out of us as when we played on the playground as children. We can recognize these places or events because they leave us breathless, dry and dusty.

Put yourself in a safe place with the Lord and allow Him to breathe on those dusty places. Focus on the presence of God as He walks through your heart, allowing Him to point out dusty places—places where you need His intimate love for yourself or someone else. Ask Him to breathe upon the dusty places again and feel the condensation of His own breath forming on you.

Experience His breath bringing new life to you. Record a list of any dusty places the Lord points out to you and how you perceive Him breathing on them.

SEE THE GLORY

Over the coming days watch to see where the Lord breathes new life and healing into your relationships and circumstances. Does He need to breathe new life into a marriage or other relationship? What about your relationship with Him? Journal about this here.

CHAPTER 7

A Restoring Love

"SINCE YOU ARE PRECIOUS IN MY SIGHT,
SINCE YOU ARE HONORED AND I LOVE YOU" (ISA. 43:4).

M any years ago, when I was in my early twenties, I was riding
with my dad in his truck through a little patch of houses near
an old coal-mining town. My father, who had been an industrial
engineer most of his life, was now at the edge of retirement and spent
a lot of time keeping his keen mind and skilled hands busy. He was a
man who could look at what most people might see as trash and see
something valuable in it. For example, Dad once salvaged a discarded
washing machine motor that became a power source for a bench
grinder. My dad saved baby food jars and coffee cans that he filled
with nuts and bolts and nails and metal stuff that I cannot identify to
this day. He would not have called himself a pack rat, but he would
say that he was putting these things "in stock" for some future need.
He had no end of projects and inventions going at any given time. He
was a man who could see something of value when others saw junk.
He had a passion for the precious.

This particular day we were driving along and my dad, the ever-
vigilant connoisseur of presently unused treasures, stopped his truck

abruptly. His eyes seemed to lock onto something important. He had spotted an old chair that was painted a ghastly yellow and lying on a heap. Dad pulled over, almost off the road, and jumped out of the truck. He plucked the chair from the heap and saw that its cane seat was missing and that there were other parts that were broken or coming apart. With chair in hand, he approached the door of the house with what could only be described as missionary zeal. Dad knocked at the door and someone answered, whereupon Dad asked if he could have the chair. (He should have taken the hint that it was unwanted, as it lay in a pile of junk.) With a bewildered look on her face, the owner of the chair agreed to let him take it. So Dad loaded his treasure carefully in the back of his truck with a look of satisfaction and purpose. He was on a mission!

When we got home, Dad took his find into his shop where parts and remnants of other chairs and strips of cane were hanging, giving his shop a jungle-like appearance. A visitor to this shop almost expected to hear tropical birds in the background! Over a period of time Dad took the old chair apart, stripped off the layers of paint and carefully wove a new cane seat for it with his own hands. Dad sometimes used an old method of applying a new finish by dipping his fingers into boiled-down linseed oil and applying it with his own hands to the bare, dry wood. There was no brush—just his bare fingers. By the time the chair was refinished, his hands and fingers had covered each dry spot with the oil, thereby restoring and transforming the discarded item into something rare and precious.

When it was reassembled, Dad had transformed it into something beautiful. He estimated that this solid walnut, handmade treasure with a ladder back and caned seat, was more than 100 years old. It was a piece that someone would probably pay a pretty penny for. They would never get the chance to do so, however, for dad never sold any of his treasures. In fact, some of Dad's recreations are in my possession today. My children will get them after I'm gone, along with a few other pieces Dad recovered in his little shop.

This old chair, destined for the landfill or the fire, became something to *sit* on. That *seat* was the nexus of my father's passion and the chair's condition. Because of the passion in his heart, Dad *saw* the discarded chair for what it really was: something precious.

PRECIOUS, HONORED, AND BELOVED

Mercy flows from the passion of the Father's heart. It has to do with what He sees in us. The Lord sees something in us that causes Him to stop his truck in front of the "junk heap" to pick us up and restore us to the vision He has of us. I'm not always sure what God sees in me or that I am of any use to Him. Nevertheless, God extends His heart and love to me in mercy and He says: "Since you are precious in My sight..." (Isa. 43:4).

What is God saying when He calls His people precious? To be precious is to be something that is rare and unique. It's probably not going to be found on the shelves at Wal-Mart. We probably can't buy it online. I'm not sure what the definition of precious is, but I know it when I see it or hold it. When I think of what is precious to me, I see the faces of my children or my grandchildren. I remember what it was like to hold them as infants, so fragile and irreplaceable. Each of them was a precious gift to us, and each is as unique as his fingerprints. They make me laugh and they make me cry. They are *precious*. When I think of what is precious, I see the face of my wife, Carol. She looks no different to me today than the day we were married. We have been together through life. She has grown more rare and precious with each passing year.

When the Lord tells us we are precious, He is saying that He sees our faces before Him as well. Each of us is a rare and precious creation. Father never tires of seeing the faces He created.

"SINCE YOU ARE HONORED..."

The Father also tells us that we are honored. To be honored is to have weight, as in weight on a scale. In the Eternal Heart, we weigh heavy, so to speak. We are no passing fancy to the One who created us.

"For we are His workmanship, created in Christ Jesus for good works, which God prepared beforehand so that we would walk in them" (Eph. 2:10). The original Greek word translated as "create" here is the word *ktizo*[1], which was originally used to refer to creating a place of habitation. We are the habitation of His Spirit and purpose. We carry the breath of the Eternal who kissed us alive and who involves us in what He is doing. We are the glory of the One who created us. There can be no greater work than this—no greater place of honor.

"I LOVE YOU..."

To be loved of God is to be the reflection of His very nature. He *is* love, as the scriptures say. The single most irrevocable and important statement within our resume is that we are loved by God! This is the greatest thing about us.

The love of the Father started in His heart and moved out toward us with no thought of the worthiness of its object. There is no *because* in the love of God for us. We can lay aside all of the reasons God loves us personally and intimately. God not only loves us, He genuinely likes us as well. We reason that He has to love us because that's who He is. But the One who created us wants to spend face time with us. He wants to see us face-to-face.

The Father not only loves us, He has what Brennan Manning referred to as a tenderness toward us. He is tender in His love. "He will be quiet in His love, He will rejoice over you with shouts of joy" (Zeph. 3:17). We bring joy to Him. Zephaniah suggests that in His love God is quiet or perhaps speechless. He is giving no reason for that love, only tender love for His heart's sake. Oh, if only we could see what He sees in us and quiet our hearts before Him in His love!

As we have ministered healing to broken hearts over these years, we have encountered precious people from every walk of life who were broken and disguised beneath layers of wounds and inaccurate self-revelation. Some had layers of failed marriages and divorce. Some were obscured by addictions or shame from some past sin. They were discarded and on the heap like that old chair my father restored. Our loving Father was not willing to allow us to stay in that condition. He replaced ashes with garlands, mourning with gladness, and fainting with praise. In one way or another, He conveyed that they were precious, honored, and beloved of God. (See Isa. 61:3.) He has a passion for the precious in us.

THE FATHER'S PASSION

We have a passionate Father. His passion toward us is not some passive sentiment. His passion wells up and moves toward its object without waiting for us to make up our minds that we miss Him. God always makes the first move toward us. We love God because He loved us first. (See 1 John 4:19.) Our passionate Father is always "on the prowl" for the precious, and He is looking for us. From the beginning, when man decided to believe a lie and was separated from God, the Father came searching for what was precious to Him saying, "Where are you?" (Gen. 3:9).

In the Old Testament, the nation of Israel was a kind of canvas upon which the passion of God for all of man was expressed. They were a people who were chosen and beloved of God (see Deut. 7:6-7), a people through whom God expressed His heart to an estranged world.

The Lord's passion for us was painted on the canvas of Israel, whom He called His inheritance—His precious possession.

> *"For the LORD's portion is His people; Jacob is the allotment of His inheritance. He found him in a desert land, And in the howling waste of a wilderness; He encircled him, He cared for him, He guarded him as the pupil of His eye. Like an eagle that stirs up its nest, that hovers over its young, He spread His wings and caught them, He carried them on His pinions"* (Deut. 32:9-11).

The Father went looking for Jacob and found him in a "desert land," a "howling waste of a wilderness." He finds us on the junk heap on the side street, unseen and unappreciated. Make no mistake; God made the first move toward Israel. Jacob was not out in the wilderness searching for God; God was holding Jacob in His hand the whole time he was lost and wandering.

We take credit for looking for God when in fact we are only responding to God's invitation. A.W. Tozer pointed out, "We pursue God because, and only because, He has first put an urge within us that spurs us to the pursuit … all the time we are pursuing God we are already in His hand."[2]

The Father refers to us with words like "precious" and "beloved." The world we live in does not see us as such. "Yes, there is a voice, the voice that speaks from above and from within and that whispers softly or declares loudly, 'You are My beloved, on you my favor rests.' It is certainly not easy to hear that voice in a world filled with voices that shout: 'You are no good; you are ugly; you are worthless; you are despicable; you are nobody—unless you can demonstrate the opposite.'"[3] The world, including the church, and we ourselves, look at the outer layer of paint and varnish and throw what has been created in tenderness and love on the junk pile. We see layers and coats made up of failure and disappointment and disqualification and forget what lies beneath—that precious, beloved child created of God—the bearer of His very breath and image.

God is a passionate Father who sees the precious in us and longs to bring us closer. Our passionate Father is moved by what He sees in us beyond the layers of sin and self-effort. We are not old, paint-covered chairs that He brings into a repair shop to refinish; we are beloved children that He brings into His Presence to undo us. In His presence, His passion for us strips away everything on the surface and touches each dry and wounded spot with the oil, the anointing of His own fingers, revealing what is precious in us.

ENDNOTES

1 *ktízo*. In Homer the word meant to found a city or a habitable place. In the NT, to create, produce from nothing. Complete Word Study New Testament…

2 A.W. Tozer, *The Pursuit of God* (Camp Hill, PA: Christian Publications), 11-12.

3 Henri J.M. Nouwen, *Life of the Beloved* (New York: Crossroad).

Turning Points

FEEL THE PASSION

Beloved, you are precious and irreplaceable to the Father from whom you came and to whom you will return for eternity. Meditate on His love for you as you read the following text aloud in a low tone until you can say it with your eyes closed. Allow the Lord to speak to you through words, images, pictures, or any other means, as you meditate on His love for you.

> *"Since you are precious in My sight, Since you are honored and I love you ..."* (Isa. 43:4).

What kinds of images of thought came to mind as you meditated on the scripture? Be sure to write them down here.

What do the images and thoughts you gathered from this scripture reveal to you about the heart of the Father? Write your thoughts here.

Now put yourself in the pictures or thoughts you received from the scripture. What is the Lord saying to you personally? Write it down here.

EXPERIENCE THE PRESENCE

Beloved, are there dry places in your life — places that need the healing oil of the Lord's lovingkindness? These are areas of your life that seem lifeless and smothered in hopelessness. They are areas where you feel unprotected and vulnerable — weathered and worn.

Seek a safe place with the Lord and allow yourself to experience the mercy of God as He finds the dry places in your heart and applies the oil of His presence with His own hand. This safe place may be one of the thoughts or images you received while meditating on the scripture above or any other place where you feel the Lord's presence. Feel the oil flowing over all the dry places.

Write down here any place in your life the Lord touches you with the healing oil of His hand.

SEE THE GLORY

Keep a journal of those dry places where you seek the personal presence of the Lord flowing over you like oil. Be sure to record the ways you sensed the Lord anointing the dry places and any further visions the Lord may grant you.

CHAPTER 8

A Present Love

Rabbi Joshua Ben-Levi once met with Elijah the prophet, and in the course of their conversation he asked, "When will Messiah come?"

"Why don't you go and ask Him yourself?" said Elijah." Where can I find Him?" the rabbi wanted to know." You will find Him sitting at the gates of Rome," answered Elijah." And how will I recognize Him?" (Or, "How will I know if it's really the Messiah?") Rabbi Joshua asked. "You will see Him among the poor, the afflicted and the diseased, binding up their wounds. However, while others bind an entire area with one bandage, the Messiah dresses each wound separately."[1]

One morning I sat with a young couple who were seeking healing from their struggles with drug addiction. They were such striking and handsome kids. Barely in their twenties, they seemed too young to be struggling with such difficult challenges. During the course of ministering to the young woman, we were able to uncover pain and lies associated with rejection. She had not grown up around a table of grace, but instead had been programmed to believe from a young age that she was the source of her mother's financial problems. Her mother blamed her daughter, because she had gotten pregnant with her at a young age and the father was just never there in her life. The Lord manifested His tenderness for this young woman during our counseling session and the couple agreed to return for ministry.

A few minutes after this "no more than a little girl" left the ministry center, she returned through the door and was sitting in the reception area hanging on to a pole, shuddering and crying with symptoms of withdrawal. Although the major reason for her condition was withdrawal from heroin, I am convinced that on some level she was looking for something more—more healing and something more eternal. When I saw her standing there crying and shivering it seemed natural to walk over to her and put my arm around her and tell her that she was loved and that these symptoms would pass. She needed more than a healing session; she needed the tangible and present love of the Father. In the midst of her pain the Father was bursting to say, *"I love you sweetheart—you are a precious gift."* His love had to be made present to the need.

Beloved, love and the mercy that expresses that love, are from God. (See 1 John 4:7.) Where mercy is, God is. Love has always been about the presence of God. From the beginning, when Adam walked with the Eternal in the Garden, to the coming of Immanuel, God with us, God's passion has been to be *with* us. This is a passion He pursues with shameless abandon.

We are a needy and helpless people when we're outside the love of God. This desperate need is like a gravitational pull on the love of the Father's heart. The Bible tells us, *"The LORD is near to the brokenhearted"* and *"a very present help."* (See Psalm 34:18 and Psalm 46:1.) He is drawn to us and our need because of His own nature. As in the Talmudic story I shared at the opening of this chapter, God, in this case the Messiah, jumps right into the middle of our needs. He is at the gates of Rome (enmeshed and mingling in the world), and He is bringing His presence and healing for each wound He sees. He is an "in your face" kind of God who gets His hands dirty on our behalf from beginning to end.

The present love of God became flesh in the person and earthly ministry of Jesus Christ. Jesus healed the blind (see Matthew 9:27-31; 20:29-34) and the lepers (see Luke 17:11-19) because His heart was disturbed—groaning with the same compassion that filled the heart of the Father. Jesus was the presence of the Father in human form—

the mercy of God walking among the needy. Jesus was what the Law of Moses aimed at but could never by itself attain. (See Galatians 3:24.)

Jesus sets forth a scenario for the present love of God by declaring that it was the fullest expression of the Kingdom of God. Jesus taught that when we minister to the need that is present before us, we minister to *Him* as well. God *is* mercy and where mercy is, God is.

THE BREAD OF HIS PRESENCE

One Sabbath day Jesus and His disciples were walking through grain fields and His disciples took a few handfuls of grain because they were hungry. Though it was the Sabbath, Jesus, the very fulfillment of the law, was not offended by their actions. The same could not be said of the religious types (the Pharisees) of His day, however. They scolded the Son of God for not keeping better control over His disciples. Jesus then related a story from the life of David through which he reminded the Pharisees that David and his men also got hungry when they were on the run from Saul's posse. Those men were given the sacred bread, the "Bread of the Presence," in order to satisfy their hunger.

When we show mercy, we are giving the bread of His presence. The heart of God is *present* in our acts of mercy. Jesus turned the tables on the religious folks by saying, "But if you had known what this means, 'I desire compassion, and not a sacrifice.'" (See Matthew 12:1-7.) He was quoting Hosea 6:6, which adds: "And in the knowledge of God rather than burnt offerings." Jesus was equating the presence of compassion or mercy with the knowledge or intimate presence of God. His point is crystal clear: Religion saw the *deed*, but mercy saw the *need*.

I believe I have been hoodwinked in the past by looking for signs and manifestations of God's presence through various kinds of dramatic demonstrations of power. In fact, simple acts of mercy were happening all around me, and went unheralded. When we love, it is with *His* love and, therefore, God is present.

On the other hand, when we minister this "present love," it is God Himself who is being ministered to. Jesus said that when we minister even to those we may deem to be unworthy, "unto the least of these," we minister to Him. (See Matthew 25:40.) How would our attitudes toward ministry change if we knew we could see the face of Jesus superimposed on the needy? I confess that many times in ministry I would like to tell people just to get over it and go home. Pretty merciful, huh?

When we love with His present and unreasonable love, we love one who carries the breath of God in them—one who is created in God's image. When we love them, we love the One whose breath they carry.

I once had a ministry session with a young woman who had been wounded over a period of years and seemed to be unable to forgive. But, as we prayed together, I suggested she try to see that it was Jesus she was ministering to—Jesus who received the mercy and forgiveness. When she was able to superimpose the face of Jesus onto the face of the offending person, she was able to forgive the other individual, and the release of compassion for her offender came immediately. She extended the present love of God to one who seemed not to deserve it and thereby freed herself from bitterness.

We are all children of the same heavenly Father. When we love people with His present love, we love Him! I think of dear Mother Teresa of Calcutta who cared for the sick and dying with honor and intimate tenderness. In one of her devotionals Mother Theresa writes:

"Lord, give me this seeing faith, then my work will never be monotonous. I will find joy in humoring the fancies and gratifying the wishes of all the poor sufferers. O beloved sick, how doubly dear you are to me, when you personify Christ; and what a privilege is mine to be allowed to tend you." [2]

We may not pick up the dying out of the gutters of Calcutta as Mother Teresa did, but the poor and dying are all around us. They are poor in that they do not know the heart of the Father who loves them with such a present and compassionate love. They are dying in the spirit for lack of this knowledge and hope. Mother Teresa is no longer here, but the Father's heart that moved and motivated her lives in us as well. She became the "present love" of the Father, ministering a love that was not her own, a love that issued from the perfect heart of the Father. She lived a love that was "from Him and through Him and to Him" (Rom. 11:36).

The present love of God, His mercy, is not given to those who *deserve* our love, but to those who *need* it. Otherwise, it is not the love of God. I do not love my children because of anything they have done to please me, but because they belong to me. I am a flawed and imperfect father and grandfather; therefore, I do not love perfectly. But our Father in Heaven is a perfect Father who loves with perfect love that eliminates fear and rejection and hurt and all the other things that rob us of peace. (See 1 John 4:18.)

When we love with mercy, the present love of God, we show whose children we are.

The mercy seat was an emblem of the Father's "present love" for His children. He is present to our need for love and our need for a personal relationship with Him and with other people, for that matter. And when we love with the Father's present love, we also establish a new order in our lives and new levels of submission to the prefect and eternal heart of Abba.

ENDNOTES

1 Chaim Pearl, *Theology of Rabbinic Stories* (Peabody, MA: Hendrickson Publishers, 1997), 145.

2 Mother Theresa, *The Joy in Loving, A Guide to Daily Living* (New York: Viking of the Penguin Group of Penguin Books USA, 1997).

3 This is a literal translation of the Hebrew text based upon margin notes in the New American Standard translation.

Turning Points

FEEL THE PASSION

God is mercy, and where mercy is present, God is present. Meditate on the following text by reading it aloud to yourself in a low voice, repeating it several times until you are able to say it with your eyes closed. Pay attention to all thoughts, words, or images that come to your mind as you meditate on the scripture.

> *God is our refuge and strength, abundantly available in tight places for help*. (Psalm 46:1)[3]

What kinds of thoughts or images come to mind as you meditate on this text? Write them here.

What do these images or thoughts communicate about the heart of God? Write your thoughts here.

Now put yourself in the pictures and thoughts you received. What is the Lord speaking to you personally?

EXPERIENCE THE PRESENCE

Recall the words of Mother Teresa, that as she ministered to the helpless she was in fact ministering to Christ. Recall now an event where you ministered in some way to a needy person whether in your family or elsewhere. This may even be a present activity or ministry. You may be washing dishes in the school cafeteria or giving an encouraging word to someone at the grocery store.

Close your eyes and now put Christ in their place. What do you see now as you minister?

SEE THE GLORY

In the days and weeks ahead keep a record of the times you have an opportunity to minister and record how you recognize Christ in those to whom you minister. How is God working through you?

CHAPTER 9

A Ransoming Love

"Salve-a-tion"

W hen I was in third or fourth grade, I saw an advertisement in one of the zillion comic books I had. It was an opportunity to win prizes such as binoculars, BB guns, real ponies, and many other things by selling a miracle-cure product that seemed to be useful for every ill known to man, from skin irritations to minor cuts and scrapes. It was called Cloverine Salve.

There was no telling how far a nine-year-old boy could go by selling this "wonder goo." I could see myself selling Cloverine Salve and not only becoming wealthy, but also doing a good thing for mankind. (Though it was probably becoming rich that really inspired me!) So I snipped out the little coupon, sent it in to the Cloverine Salve Company and waited for the product to be delivered to my doorstep.

After a couple of weeks, lo and behold, my inventory arrived. I opened the box and was greeted by the aroma of healing that smelled like a blend of my Dad's Old Spice aftershave and some kind of toothache medicine. Here were twelve to fourteen tins and a bill for something like five dollars to be paid when I sold the wonder salve. I think the price per tin was thirty-five cents. I was now in business and in debt to the Cloverine Salve Company!

I tucked the sample box under my arm and proceeded to go out to heal the neighborhood. Here I was: a husky, nine-year-old huckster with a freckled face, a fresh summer crew cut, and a box of healing under my arm. What could be more impressive? I went from door to door down the street with my best smile and sales pitch and a "can't miss" attitude. It was only a matter of time until I would be a great success and a credit to my family! But after visiting most of the houses on our block, I did not sell a single tin of Cloverine Salve!

This effort was repeated for the next several days, but I only managed to sell one or two tins. What would I do with the other ten, and where would the money come from to pay off my debt? Arghh! It was pretty hard for a kid to save four dollard when I got only fifty cents a week! That could wreck my whole summer. I began to envision myself being dragged away from my family in chains by the Cloverine Salve people to an uncertain end of servitude in the salve mines of some remote island. It was a dismal prospect.

I'm not sure how or when, but Dad somehow noticed the sackcloth and ashes I was wearing around and asked me what was wrong. I told him about my debt and dilemma. And as Dad did so many times, he put his hand in his own pocket and took out the few dollars required to remove the yoke of balm-bondage from my neck. Dad paid the full price and bought all the salve himself. I sent the ransom in as fast as I could put a four-cent stamp on an envelope. Needless to say, the burden lifted as Dad came through for me once again. I never did find out what he did with all that salve.

RANSOMING LOVE

Mercy is like the "ransom" that was paid by my dad for me. The word we translate as "mercy seat" in Hebrew is *kapporeth*, which points toward the concept of covering. The Hebrew root, *kaphar*, is a word that indicates either a covering, as in throwing a garment or covering over us, and at the same time covering, as in paying a ransoming price.[1] Both are part of the mercy seat. In His ransoming love, the Father does both things in that He covers our naked and helpless condition and also provides a way to cover the cost of our captivity to sin and self. Outside of mercy, the ransoming love of God, we have no hope of coming near to God.

When we think of ransom, we think of someone who has been taken captive and a villain or terrorist who requires payment to release and return them to their loved ones. In this case, we are held captive by our own decisions to sin. Nobody bound and gagged me to make me sin. I went with my captors willingly and allowed them to put their chains and constraints on me, yet God puts His hands in His own "pockets" and pays the price to cover my sin, even with the cost of His own Son.

We are as hopeless as the nine-year-old boy who was indentured to the salve company. You and I are stuck—held captive and in need of redemption. We are powerless to do anything unless God makes the first move, and He did so by sending His son, Jesus Christ. Christ became the mercy seat—the ransom. "In this is love, not that we loved God, but that He loved us and sent His Son to be the **propitiation** for our sins" (1 John 4:10, NKJV, emphasis mine). The word translated "propitiation" in the Scripture is the Greek word *hilasmos*.[2] It is the same word translated as "mercy seat" in the Septuagint (the Greek Old Testament translation).

From His own mouth we know that ransoming lost man was the reason why Jesus came to earth. He says, "For even the Son of Man did not come to be served, but to serve, and to give His life a **ransom** for many" (Mark 10:45, NKJV, emphasis mine). (See also 1 Timothy 2:5-6.) There is no power in heaven or on earth that cannot be broken by the mercy of God, not even death itself. God said to Israel, "I will **ransom** them from the power of the grave; I will redeem them from death" (Hos. 13:14, NIV, emphasis mine).

I think of C.S. Lewis' *The Lion, the Witch, and the Wardrobe* in which Edmund was taken captive by the White Witch, was found guilty of treason, and was sentenced to death. But instead, Aslan goes willingly to the table of the Law and allows himself to be bound and beaten and shaved, then finally murdered in Edmund's place. It was mercy, the ransoming love of God, that allowed Aslan to be tied to that table and that permitted Edmund to go free. Ultimately, it was mercy, "the deeper magic" that overwhelmed all the power of the White Witch just as Jesus overcame all the power of sin and Satan.

COVERING LOVE

God is a covering God. Mercy is the divine instinct. When man was willfully disobedient and separated from God in the Garden, the Father provided the covering of animal hides as an act of mercy. (See Genesis 3:21.) Out of His own love and initiative, the Father made a way to bring Adam out of the bushes and back to His heart.

At the mercy seat, sins were covered or blotted out by the application of blood from animal sacrifices. God instructed Moses to have the priest offer sweet-smelling incense that would cloud over the mercy seat just as the cloud covered Sinai; perhaps this was meant to serve as a reminder of the eternal embrace and revelation of the Father's heart Moses had experienced on the mountain. The Father always wanted to bring us back to the revelation of His heart, which was filled with compassion and manifested in mercy.

Once the glory cloud of incense was formed, the priest was to take some of the blood of animals that were slain in sacrifice for sins and sprinkle it on the mercy seat. (See Leviticus 16:12-16.) This blood represented not only a covering for sin but also the ransom price for the return of the people to the presence of God. It was all about bringing His people back into His presence and embrace.

Despite all of our failures and flops our Father's heart is always to cover us with His mercy. Consider the story Jesus told of the Prodigal Son and the loving father.

> *"A man had two sons. The younger of them said to his father, 'Father, give me the share of the estate that falls to me.' So he divided his wealth between them.*
>
> *"And not many days later, the younger son gathered everything together and went on a journey into a distant country, and there he squandered his estate with loose living. Now when he had spent everything, a severe famine occurred in that country, and he began to be impoverished. So he went and hired himself out to one of the citizens of that country, and*

he sent him into his fields to feed swine. And he would have gladly filled his stomach with the pods that the swine were eating, and no one was giving anything to him.

"But when he came to his senses, he said, 'How many of my father's hired men have more than enough bread, but I am dying here with hunger! I will get up and go to my father, and will say to him, "Father, I have sinned against heaven, and in your sight; I am no longer worthy to be called your son; make me as one of your hired men."' So he got up and came to his father.

"But while he was still a long way off, his father saw him and felt compassion for him, and ran and embraced him and kissed him.

"And the son said to him, 'Father, I have sinned against heaven and in your sight; I am no longer worthy to be called your son.'

"But the father said to his slaves, 'Quickly bring out the best robe and put it on him, and put a ring on his hand and sandals on his feet; and bring the fattened calf, kill it, and let us eat and celebrate; for this son of mine was dead and has come to life again; he was lost and has been found'" (Luke 15:11-24).

This story in Luke 15 represents the passionate and broken-hearted love of the eternal Father for His children who go off on their own trying to find something that was never lost: their precious value. The first thing the father did, upon welcoming the son back into his embrace, was to call for a covering. *He said, Quickly go get the robe* (Luke 15:22). That robe had been hanging in the closet since the boy left home. It was handmade to fit this son. The only thing the boy had to do was to return to the father's covering embrace.

It's amazing and tragic how we humans frequently add something to the covering love of the Father. Notice that the loving father did not say, "Son, I can see that you have had a change of heart, but now in order to live with me you need to go through some discipleship classes on how to be a good son, how to raise sheep and not smell like them," or something like that. The father sent for the robe and threw it over his son's back. We might think that it would be up to the son who came to the end of himself to live up to the robe that was so tenderly thrown on his back. In reality, however, it was not up to him. This son was "re-covered" by the father. It was the love of that gracious father that changed the heart of the son. The son remembered what his father was like, and when he remembered the heart of his father and how his father treated his servants, he turned from the pigpen and back to the father's embrace

I have seen this so many times in ministry. Many people don't feel "good enough" for God. The truth is that we aren't good enough for God, but His own goodness, as seen in the mercy that covers us, makes us good in His eyes.

Recently I was ministering in a church where a leader had admitted a struggle with secret sin and had stepped away from ministry, for a period of time. The response to this open struggle with sin was amazing in that now those who had felt too imperfect for God were coming home to the church. The man had been asked many times to speak to a group of men, but he always declined because of his own secret sin. When this man of God humbled himself and confessed his struggles, he finally had nothing to hide and agreed to speak to the groups only as a man, not a leader.

The result was that many came to the same place of humility and received the mercy of God. They had all accepted the ransom that was paid, the covering robe that was offered. This child of God was restored in the covering love of the Father and was now ready to throw covering over others who were out in the cold and far from home. They now felt safe beneath the covering love of the Father who had so lovingly restored this son.

Covering love originates in the heart of God, yet we resist the embrace of the Father and try to cover ourselves.

"SELF-COVERING"

We often try to cover our nakedness or pay our own ransom. Just as Adam and Eve did, we weave fig leaves together of self-covering. They may be fig leaves of good works or fig leaves of religion or maybe fig leaves of perfectionism. But in the end they all come unraveled and we are exposed and powerless. If we do not find our mercy seat in Christ, we will try to do something to become sufficient in ourselves. We call this self-covering or self-righteousness.

Covering ourselves in self-righteousness is the greatest sin there is, because it keeps us from the presence of God where we were created to live in fellowship and intimate communion. Therefore, if we are indulging ourselves in self-righteousness in some way, in any way, and try to cover ourselves, we are putting a barrier between us and God. Whatever we clothe ourselves with, the Father is going to have to remove from us. We cannot clothe ourselves in titles. We can't clothe ourselves in performance or works or appearance or any other thing. Anything we rely upon other than the covering love of the Father in Christ will become an obstacle and a barrier that separates us from the Father.

Self-righteousness is chiefly about forgetting God. In Deuteronomy 8:14 God warns Israel about this. It's as if He's saying, *Watch out, that when you come into the promised land—that I, by the way, got for you—that you forget that it was Me that brought you there in the first place. You will become proud in your own heart* (author's paraphrase). Again, anything we put on, the Father has to take off. Anything that we try to do to accomplish righteousness, He is going to have to remove from us.

Isaiah 64:6 says, "For all of us have become like one who is unclean, and all our righteous deeds are like a filthy garment." We need to allow the Father to throw His covering love over us and to live like children of God. Jesus came to make a new and living way back to the heart of the Father so that we would turn away from meaningless, self-covering efforts.

God is a covering, loving Father who longs to bring us to His heart. The Father put His hands in His own pockets and paid the ransom out of His own glory through His Son, Jesus Christ. He calls us His children, covers us with His own blood, and calls us near to His intimate presence.

But now in Christ Jesus you who formerly were far off have been brought near by the blood of Christ (Eph. 2:13).

A question comes to my mind as I write these words. I wonder how many souls I am holding hostage because of their offenses against me. We hold others for ransom as well until they are sufficiently penitent to deserve our forgiveness. If I have accepted the mercy of God and have been set free by the ransom He paid, and if I am living under the robe He has provided, how can I still require something more from someone who has offended me? We are all under the same robe!

"Lord, give us the grace to turn toward mercy in our dealings with those who have offended us and bring them, too, under your warm, robe of covering love—your mercy."

ENDNOTES

1 *Theological Wordbook of the Old Testament* (Chicago: Moody Press, 1980), 452-453.
2 NT:2434 *hilasmos* (hil-as-mos'); atonement, i.e. (concretely) an expiator: KJV - propitiation.
(Biblesoft's New Exhaustive Strong's Numbers and Concordance with Expanded Greek-Hebrew Dictionary. Copyright (c) 1994, Biblesoft and International Bible Translators, Inc.)

Turning Points

FEEL THE PASSION

Beloved, the price has been paid for all. Meditate on this scripture by reading it aloud in a low tone until you can repeat it with your eyes closed. Allow the Lord to speak to you in words, thoughts, images or in any other way that He desires to reveal His heart to you.

[Jesus] Himself is the propitiation [mercy seat, ransom price, covering] for our sins; and not for ours only, but also for those of the whole world (1 John 2:2).

What kinds of thoughts or images come to mind as you meditate on this scripture? Write them down here.

What do the images and scriptures reveal about the heart of God? Write your thoughts here.

Now put yourself in the pictures and thoughts. What is the Lord saying to you personally?

EXPERIENCE THE PRESENCE

Are there places in your life where you are trying to pay your own ransom—to cover yourself? Beloved, the price has been paid for all. There is no more explaining or covering that must be done, only accept the ransoming love of the Father provided in His Son, Jesus Christ. Place yourself in a safe place with the presence of the Lord and allow Him to help you find any part of your life or heart where you feel as though you are in over your head. Allow yourself to experience His rescuing grace—to reveal to you the ransom price He has paid for you.

Write down any thoughts, words or visions the Lord may give to you as He covers you in ransoming love.

SEE THE GLORY

Keep a journal in the coming days of any place or event where you realize you have been covering yourself –where you try to earn love and acceptance. Then allow the Lord to remind you that He has paid the ransom. Experience freedom as you release yourself to the love of God.

CHAPTER 10

A Sovereign Love

There once was a good and righteous king who lived in a great palace situated on the summit of a lofty mountain. This king donned a purple robe that was thick and warm; it blended the blue colors of the mountain with the red of the land below. A golden, bejeweled crown rested on his royal brow, declaring his sovereign reign over his kingdom.

The robe hung heavily on the king's broad and regal shoulders, weighed down with his own goodness. It was scented with the fragrance of the king's garden. The fragrance would waft out from time to time, carried by the breeze that came off the mountain and into the surrounding country.

This regal sovereign sat on a throne of gold that was radiant with his glory. No corner of his vast hall was obscured from his great glory and goodness. From that exalted throne the king looked and was able to see the land below through an open gate. Crumpled by the gate at the foot of the mountain was a man who was dressed in rags that carried another kind of a scent, that of hopelessness and discouragement. He sat cold and alone, nearly naked in ragged clothing, soiled with the stains of self-effort and futile failure and looking up to the mountain toward the throne of the king. The beggar sat at the gate with his face bowed toward the king; he had been immobilized by hopelessness and was unable to move from his position under his own power.

Now clothed in his heavy robe from his throne, the king looked beyond the radiance of his throne and saw the naked beggar at the gate. The king's heart was so moved with compassion at the sight of the man's face, he rose up and walked down the mountain, leaving an empty throne behind. As the king approached the beggar, the man of the lowland caught the scent of the precious and sweet resin that clung to the heavy purple robe of the king and hung down his head.

Now, as the good king came near to the naked beggar, he lifted up the beggar's head, cupping his worn and weary face into his hands and looking deeply into his eyes. Seeing his helpless estate, the heart of the king was moved. Then, in one sweeping motion, the king untied his robe and threw it over the shoulders of the man at the gate, smell and all. The king uncovered himself in order to cover the cold and dirty figure who lived by the gate.

The king was no less a king for this gesture of sovereign compassion. The king's throne and fragrance now filled the land below.

> *For thus says the high and exalted One Who lives forever, whose name is Holy, "I dwell on a high and holy place, And also with the contrite and lowly of spirit In order to revive the spirit of the lowly And to revive the heart of the contrite"* (Isa. 57:15).

MERCY: THE THRONE OF HEAVEN AND EARTH

A *crown*, a *throne*, and a *robe* are all expressions of mercy, the sovereign love of God. It was at the mercy seat that heaven met earth and where the Sovereign Heart of heaven set up His throne and expressed His passion to be among His people. We are naked and helpless beggars standing at the gate.

As the Lord gave instructions to build the mercy seat, it was to be set upon the Ark, which had a golden crown around it, giving it the unmistakable appearance that the mercy seat was surrounded by a crown.

And thou shalt overlay it [the ark] with pure gold, within and without shalt thou overlay it, and shalt make upon it a crown of gold round about (Exod. 25:11, KJV).

The mercy seat held the very crown that was on the eternal brow. The crown around the mercy seat is a statement that God is enthroned in the midst of mercy. When mercy is shown, the reign of God is seen.

Mercy is the entourage of His royal glory that goes before Him and declares His sovereignty. "Righteousness and justice are the foundation of Your throne; Lovingkindness [mercy] and truth go before You" (Ps. 89:14). We are not able to encounter the awesome righteousness of God before we encounter the mercy of God. In the mercy seat the Father made a way for us who are naked at the gate to have access to His throne.

Mercy flows out of sovereign authority. Only the completely sovereign and secure can be completely merciful. God is sovereign, and He has a right to invite anyone He wants into His presence. What a thrill and an honor. He has invited us! If we refuse His invitation, we contend with the sovereign love of God. He is a King who changes us as He draws us close.

The Father is not an insecure deity fashioned by our hands and imaginations, who needs appeasement and constant reassurance of His power and authority. Because God is totally sovereign, He can be totally merciful. Consider this picture in the Book of Esther; it is when Esther comes into the presence of the king, a crime punishable by instant death.

When the king saw Esther the queen standing in the court, she obtained favor in his sight; and the king extended to Esther the golden scepter which was in his hand. So Esther came near and touched the top of the scepter (Esther 5:2).

As Esther entered the throne room, the king extended his scepter and she was permitted to touch this symbol of total sovereign authority preserving her life. Mercy flows from authority, and it is extended by the sovereign will of the one who holds the power of life and death. It is extended only to those who humble themselves at His feet, recognizing His sovereignty and their helplessness.

Mercy, a sovereign love, requires a Sovereign. I cannot be both sovereign and subject at the same time. If we have submitted ourselves to the throne of heaven and have come under the covering of its mercy, then we are under the same robe as those with whom we hold accounts. Recall the unrighteous servant whom the king forgave millions, the one who had persecuted others for hundreds. The money was not his in the first place, but it was the king's. (See Matthew 18:23-35.) The accounts we hold are not ours if we belong to the King; they are His.

We humans tend to think that showing mercy makes us weak, but, in fact, showing mercy is an indication that we are secure under the hand of God. When we extend mercy, we are extending the rule of God's heart in us. When we live under the rule of God's sovereign love, we are no longer subject to mere justice. We have been seated with God, and from that position we extend the love and compassion that is needed to bring healing rather than just fairness.

When Jesus refers to the kingdom of heaven or the kingdom of God, He is referring to the sovereignty of God in the here and now, not just some eschatological kingdom in the future. The reign of God has come among us and flows through us as we turn our faces toward mercy for ourselves and the others who wait at the gate, hopeless and separated from the throne of God.

AN EMPTY THRONE

Seeing our neediness, the King's heart was full and His throne empty as He descended to heal our naked and beggarly condition at the gate. Jesus emptied the throne He once filled and made the decision to throw His robe over us.

> *Have this attitude in yourselves which was also in Christ Jesus, who, although He existed in the form of God, did not regard equality with God a thing to be grasped, but **emptied Himself**...He **humbled Himself** by becoming obedient to the point of death, even death on a cross. For this reason also, God highly exalted Him, and bestowed on Him the name which is*

above every name, so that at the name of Jesus every knee will bow, of those who are in heaven and on earth and under the earth, and that every tongue will confess that Jesus Christ is Lord, to the glory of God the Father (Phil. 2:5-11, author's paraphrase of NASB).

Jesus, as God and King, left behind an empty throne and came walking into the middle of our irreconcilable problems with relationships and our struggles with sin. He throws His robe over us and loves us simply because we are His. The mercy of God is not for sale; it is not a right or a universal grant, but an act of the sovereign will of the King to all who turn their bowed faces toward His face.

Mercy is the proof that the kingdom of heaven has arrived and waits to be set up all around us. Consider the many around us with broken hearts and broken families. They are lost in this post-modern, politically correct spiritual anarchy and crying out to a brassy heaven. We are the ones over whom the King has elected to throw His robe, the ones to whom He is bringing the fragrance of Christ.

That fragrance is the same one as applied to the priests of His presence in the Old Testament in Exodus 30:23, the chief ingredient of which was myrrh. Myrrh was also used upon the bodies of he dead to defer the smell of corruption. Myrrh was the aroma of death.

Our King was presented with such myrrh from His birth. Upon His birth the fragrance of the King's love wafted out of heaven to the nostril of the needy: us!

THE SOVEREIGN PLAN OF GOD

I have seen the sovereign love of God through many healing sessions, as the King has come to lead the wounded out of the bondage of hurt and past abuse and into His healing embrace. Consider one young man who lived in many foster homes throughout his life. He became dependent on drugs as a teenager in his attempt to anesthetize the pain of his loneliness. His parents had been killed before his eyes as a very small child. He was alone and desperate for love.

As we revisited the scene of his parents' death, where the little boy felt alone and powerless, the King once again left His throne and threw His robe over the little boy. The young man began to realize that the King had sovereignly led him to a healing encounter with His presence.

Because the Lord is sovereign, He leads us to His feet where we can be healed. He has been leading us into His embrace all our lives, though we have not always been aware of His invitation.

One evening I sat with a woman and her husband. The wife had been terrorized and molested by her father as a little girl. As we approached one of those horrific frames from the past, the woman was unable to recognize or acknowledge the presence of the Lord. But the Lord in His relentless love continued to draw the wounded, little child to a safe place in Himself, and He drew her into a sweet embrace that brought healing to her wounded child within. Both the child and the woman were safe in the embrace of the Lord. As the healing session unfolded, we were able to see that the Lord had been leading her to this moment of healing all her life. He had gently led her to the mercy seat and into His embrace.

Such tenderness flows from the heart of the King who emptied His throne and came in love to bring us back into intimate union with Himself. The King has emptied His throne and cast off His own robe and thrown it across our backs to cover our nakedness. Mercy is the sovereign love of God and the love of the Sovereign for all of us at His gates. As we receive and live in mercy, the aroma of the King fills the nostrils of the needy.

Turning Points

FEEL THE PASSION

Beloved, the Sovereign Majesty of Heaven longs to take our faces in His hands and reveal His love for us.

Meditate on the following verse by reading it to yourself in a low tone several times until you can say it with your eyes closed.

> *But thanks be to God, who always leads us in triumph in Christ, and manifests through us the sweet aroma of the knowledge of Him in every place* (2 Cor. 2:14).

Allow the Lord to speak to you through images, words and thoughts as He extends His sovereign love to you. Be sure to write down what the Lord communicates to you.

What do the scriptures and the images that came to mind reveal to you about the heart of the King?

What do you sense the Lord communicating about His heart toward you personally as you meditated on the scriptures?

EXPERIENCE THE PRESENCE

Beloved, the Sovereign Majesty of Heaven longs to reveal His love for us. The fragrance of that love is released from His holy mountain as we meditate on Him. Fix your eyes upon Jesus, the King enthroned, and allow yourself to be surrounded by the precious fragrance of the King's robes. Let the pungent sweetness of the myrrh waft over you. Breathe it into your spiritual lungs. What does that fragrance smell like to you? Can you smell it?

Write your description of His fragrant love here along with any other images or thoughts that come to mind as you breathe in His presence and peace.

SEE THE GLORY

Keep a journal in the next few days of places where you surrender to the sovereignty of God. Take note of those occasions when you are aware of the fragrant love of God's sovereign love around you—where you see yourself or others stuck at the gate unable to move as the beggar in the story.

CHAPTER 11

A Transforming Love

THEN HE SHOWED ME JOSHUA THE HIGH PRIEST STANDING BEFORE THE ANGEL OF THE LORD, AND SATAN STANDING AT HIS RIGHT HAND TO ACCUSE HIM. THE LORD SAID TO SATAN, "THE LORD REBUKE YOU, SATAN. INDEED, THE LORD WHO HAS CHOSEN JERUSALEM REBUKE YOU. IS THIS NOT A BRAND PLUCKED FROM THE FIRE." NOW JOSHUA WAS CLOTHED WITH FILTHY GARMENTS AND STANDING BEFORE THE ANGEL. HE SPOKE AND SAID TO THOSE WHO WERE STANDING BEFORE HIM, SAYING, "REMOVE THE FILTHY GARMENTS FROM HIM." AGAIN HE SAID TO HIM, "SEE, I HAVE TAKEN YOUR INIQUITY AWAY FROM YOU AND WILL CLOTHE YOU WITH FESTAL ROBES." THEN I SAID, "LET THEM PUT A CLEAN TURBAN ON HIS HEAD." SO THEY PUT A CLEAN TURBAN ON HIS HEAD AND CLOTHED HIM WITH GARMENTS, WHILE THE ANGEL OF THE LORD WAS STANDING BY (ZECHARIAH 3:1-5).

Imagine this scene, painted by the prophet Zechariah. Joshua, the high priest of Israel, stood before a throne of brilliant gold emblazoned with eternal and unquenchable fire and holiness. The throne sat on a floor that looked like precious gemstones, but was as clear as the sky on its bluest day. The throne of heaven was surrounded by fiery angels who covered the presence of the One who sat upon it. At the same time the throng of heaven sang a continuous antiphonal praise to the holiness and glory of the One who dwelt in unapproachable light. The atmosphere around the throne was filled with the sweet scent of something like cassia and cinnamon. It was a vision of utter purity and light, enthroned and filling every sense and beyond.

There was a robe around the One who sat on the throne; it trailed off His back, filled the space before Him and extended out in every direction until it disappeared. (See Isaiah 6:1.) This robe was the essence of the Eternal going out to touch everything in the throne room of heaven.

Now into this brilliant scene stepped a figure who was out of place among the retinue of heaven. He had no brilliance or light—nothing that placed him here in the midst of such eternal, brilliant perfection. Instead, he was covered in filthy rags, defiling every sense that existed in the ultra-purity of heaven. How could the Pure and the putrid exist in the same space? God is light and there is not one speck of darkness or impurity in Him. He will not abide nor accommodate such defilement. Someone had to change, and it could not be the Unchangeable One.

OUR STANDING BEFORE GOD

This is one of the visions of the prophet Zechariah, who is seen here prophesying to a recovering nation. The people of God had been sent into captivity for seventy years because of their hardness of heart and idolatry and at the same time because of the Father's desire to purify the nation. Now the people were returning to reclaim the place where the Name was pleased to dwell.

The vision in Zechariah 3 describes the standing of a nation before God with the high priest as its chief representative. It also gives us an idea of the Father's heart toward us who stand in His presence by our own strength with no hope of restoration. We come into the presence of God as Joshua did, wearing "filthy garments"; literally "dung-spattered rags."[1] The only thing that will allow us to remain in His presence is mercy: the transforming love of God.

We are not alone before the throne of God. Satan is there to jog our memories and give voice to our failings and sins. An inner voice in our heads replays condemning, toxic tapes that point to our "filthiness" before God—reminding us of where we have blown it and where the weaknesses and low spots in our walls are to be found. Satan, whose name describes his role as "the accuser," stands before the angel of the Lord trying to keep us separated from the Father's heart by any means possible. He presents his case against us as the DA from hell. When he has presented all of his evidence, we stand mute before the beatific bench, just as Joshua did, because we are in fact *guilty*. Everything he says about us, as he reminds us of our shortfalls, is true. We are caught and paralyzed in our own stink.

The Angel of the Lord is Christ, who represents us as we stand naked before our accuser. Jesus ever lives to make intercession for us. (See Hebrews 7:25.) He takes His stand between us and our accuser. Christ is not a defense attorney, as there is no kind of defense for us. He will not put up an argument or present our case or even cross-examine the devil. We, as Joshua was, are standing clothed in the defiling evidence, and we have no other course but to admit our desperate need and throw ourselves on the mercy of the court. We have nothing in us, with which to clothe ourselves including our good works and empty religion. In fact, the works we've done in self-righteousness actually add to the smell of our uncleanness. "For all of us have become like one who is unclean, And all our righteous deeds are like a filthy garment" (Isa. 64:6). Though we don't like to mention these things in our post-modern Christianity anymore, we have to realize that we are a mess.

Just when the verdict should come in to give us our just deserts, the voice of the Father thunders over Heaven's bench and says, "I, the Lord, reject your accusations, satan. Yes, the Lord who has chosen Jerusalem [You can take out Jerusalem and put your name in its place.] ... This one has been snatched from the fire."

We, like Joshua, have been "snatched from the fire" and the destructive power of sin and unrighteousness. God has not denied our sin nor has He denied His own righteousness or put it on hold.

Zechariah says that the Lord "rejected" or refused the accusations against us, pushing them away and rebuking the accuser.

It needs to be said that you and I are not helpless victims of sin; we are willing participants in it. We took those dung-spattered rags out of the stinky closet of sin and put them on. But we are created to live in the intimate embrace of the Father and He is not willing to leave us outside where we cannot stink up His throne room. Neither will He pull out some kind of celestial air freshener. He is not content to leave things the way they are.

So ... since we are helpless to change ourselves, He is going to change us like babies with dirty diapers. One of the biggest words in this biblical text is so. The word "so" eliminates all empty, self-serving, powerless religion with just two letters. We are filthy and defiled and unable to change on our own, "so" God is going to do something about it. We have nothing to do with it but to submit to His transforming love.

Here in the presence of pure love the Father says, "Take off his filthy clothes. And turning to Joshua he said, 'See, I have taken away your sins, and now I am giving you these fine new clothes'" (Zech. 3:4, NLT).

Psalm 109:30-31 says, "With my mouth I will give thanks abundantly to the Lord; And in the midst of many I will praise Him." Why? Read verse 31: "For He stands at the right hand of the needy." We are the "needy," and Jesus is at our right hand! The Lord, the ascended Christ, came down from His throne and took His stand at our right hand in order to become our Advocate and our Sufficiency. He emptied His throne and took His place at our side to make intercession for us.

What did Joshua do to achieve this transformation? He got into the presence of God. Where does this leave religion? Where does this leave performance? Where does this leave self-righteousness? All of them together are laid aside in one smelly heap.

The Angel of the Lord said, "See, I have taken away your sins." He has removed our filthiness and sin. He has removed everything that could keep us out of His presence, where we were created to live. In the text it doesn't even seem to me that Joshua was even ready to surrender his filthiness. Joshua had enough faith, however, to respond to the invitation of the Lord to turn his face toward His presence. When he came into the presence of the Lord, the Lord stepped down out of His place and literally undressed him—took the filthy rags from him and removed them.

CHANGED IN HIS PRESENCE

The scriptures say the kindness of God leads us to repentance (Rom. 2:4). The Father draws us with mercy or lovingkindness. (See Jeremiah 31:3.) It is in the presence and the heart of God to remove the filth of "fallenness" and then dress us in a new, clean garment arrayed with His own festal brilliance. We are literally changed, transformed in His presence, or maybe we could say His presence changes us. And His presence is manifested and expressed in mercy that leads us back to Him, as He imputes His own righteousness to us on the basis of His own heart. (See James 2:23.)

Once we have been arrayed in the King's own robe, He also gives us a new turban—a new mind to match the garment on our backs. Oh, how we would live differently in the presence of the One who calls us to Himself. As the Spirit of the Lord works within us, we become more and more like him and reflect his glory even more. (See 2 Cor. 3:18.)

God has imputed (literally "covered" us) with His own garment, as the scriptures say: "I will rejoice greatly in the LORD, My soul will exult in my God; For He has clothed me with garments of salvation, He has wrapped me with a robe of righteousness" (Isa. 61:10); and "For all of you who were baptized into Christ have clothed yourselves with Christ" (Gal. 3:27). (See also Rom. 13:14.)

Our desire to be in the presence of the Lord started with Him. He changes our hearts as His transforming love flows from His throne to allow us to live in the embrace of His presence. In that embrace is a further promise for the One whose garments we wear.

*Thus says the LORD of hosts, "If you will **walk in My ways** and if you will **perform My service**, then you will also govern My house and also have charge of My courts, and I will grant you free access among these who are standing here* (Zech 3:7, emphasis mine).

The Lord promises us that we will have free access to His presence if we will "walk in His ways" and "perform His service." How much easier it is to walk in His ways or to follow Him once we have experienced His heart. It is then that we follow Him in reverential joy rather than terror or fear.

I recall the day after I came to the knowledge that the Lord loved me personally and I prayed to affirm that unreasonable love. I did not know what to do with it all. I had grown up in a traditional Lutheran home where religion had its place, but where we did not speak of this newfound rapture in the heart of God. I used to try to make it from communion to communion, where sin would be dealt with by receiving the sacraments. I remember those days in the Lutheran church with great fondness, because that is where I learned the Bible stories that now have come alive to me. They were made up of real, struggling people like me—folks who had the stink of the world on them, but who were also transformed by the love of the Father's heart.

The morning after my conversion to the mercy of God, I was driving an old VW bug through the mountains of western Pennsylvania, and I was thinking about what had happened the night before. There was a lingering sense of God's personal invested presence surrounding me, though I would not have called it that in those days. Frankly I didn't know what to call it. But as I drove and remembered my prayer on the living room floor of the home of my Alliance pastor friend, my heart began to overflow. I felt like singing, though I did not know what to sing. I had never heard a praise chorus or even knew there was such a thing. All I could think of were various parts of the Lutheran liturgy and the Catholic mass, which I had learned while I was in St. Vincent College as an undergraduate. All at once, the words I had sung since childhood by rote began to flood from my mouth while my VW beetle was filled with the glory of God as surely as it had covered Mount Sinai. I sang out, "My soul doth magnify the Lord, and my spirit hath rejoiced in God my Saviour" (Luke 1:46-47, KJV). I had no idea where the words had come from, but they now resonated in my heart and flowed from my mouth as a fountain of praise from deep within me.

God had invited me to "Come up here and live," and I had accepted His gracious invitation. I was overwhelmed and forced to pull over so I could weep tears of ecstatic joy, as the Spirit of God rejoiced with me. (I did not know there even was a Holy Spirit at that time!)

The Lord had changed my garments and given me His own righteous, festal robes. Did I stop sinning from that point on? Did I walk in perfect holiness? Sadly, no. Not even close. It would be years until I would be discipled in the truth that flooded my heart those many years ago. I went through many other trials in the perfecting of my faith. But through it all, the Lord has not taken His garments from me. I wear them today in humility—and the garments are as fresh as that first moment when He clothed me.

The Lord Himself has drawn us, covered us, and changed us in His presence, according to mercy, His transforming love, and now, nothing shall separate us from the love of God which is in Christ Jesus (Rom. 8:39).

Endnotes

1 OT:6674. "tsow" (tso); from an unused root meaning to issue; soiled. KJV— filthy. (Biblesoft's *New Exhaustive Strong's Numbers and Concordance with Expanded Greek-Hebrew Dictionary*. Copyright (c) 1994, Biblesoft and International Bible Translators, Inc.)

Turning Points

FEEL THE PASSION

Beloved, you are safe in the heart of God, as you turn toward Him in simple trust. Meditate on the following scripture verse by reading it to yourself aloud in a low tone until you can say it with your eyes closed. As you speak these words over yourself, pay attention to any words, images, or thoughts that come to your mind.

For all of you who were baptized into Christ have clothed yourselves with Christ (Gal. 3:27).

What kinds of thoughts or images came to mind as you meditated on the scriptures? Write them down here.

What do these words or images reveal to you about the heart of God and His transforming love? Record your impressions here.

What is the Lord speaking to you personally through these words, images and scriptures? Put yourself in the thoughts and images He has given to you and write His personal word to you here.

EXPERIENCE THE PRESENCE

Beloved, you are safe in the heart of God as you turn toward Him in simple trust. Allow yourself to enter the throne room of heaven in the presence of the Almighty One. As you stand before the King of Heaven there may be words of accusation coming from somewhere inside you. Record any words that come to mind, then allow the Lord to silence the accuser and to put His own garments of celebration on you.

As you experience the personal presence of God silencing the accuser write down anything you sense the Lord speaking to you from His throne of grace as you stand before Him.

SEE THE GLORY

Over the coming days record times when you feel exposed or condemned. Write down the words the Lord uses to replace that negative, accusing self-talk with His covering love.

CHAPTER 12

An Embracing Love

"THE CHERUBIM SHALL HAVE THEIR WINGS SPREAD UPWARD,
COVERING THE MERCY SEAT" (EXOD. 25:20A).

Mercy and the mercy seat flow from the *passion* and represent the *presence* of God's heart. Mercy begins in the intimate, inner chambers of the Father's heart, then reaches out to gather us back into His passionate embrace. The mercy of God is ultimately the *embracing love* of God.

IN THE SHADOW OF HIS WINGS

Among the striking features of the mercy seat is the awesome image of two cherubim at each end with their wings overshadowing the throne of God. (See Hebrews 9:5.) Cherubim are covering angels who attend or accompany the presence of God. At the mercy seat, the overshadowing wings of the cherubim form a place of intimate embrace in the very heart of God.

The overshadowing of mercy, the Father's embracing love, resembles Brennan Manning's description of solitude:

In solitude [within the embracing love of the Father] we listen with great attentiveness to the voice that calls us beloved. God speaks to the deepest strata of our souls, into our self-hatred and shame, our narcissism, and takes us through the night in the daylight of his truth: "Do not be afraid, for I have redeemed you; I have called you by name, you are mine. You are precious in my eyes, because you are honored and I love you ... the mountains may depart, the hills be shaken, but my love for you will never be shaken" (Isa. 43:1, 54:10).[1]

Beneath the shadow of covering wings, we are safe and secreted away with Him, as we are drawn into a warm embrace within the heart of the Father just as infants are wrapped in the love of their parents.

Awhile back I was visiting in our daughter Amy's house before I left on a ministry trip. She had prepared a lunch for us, and we sat on her front porch to eat together in an alfresco manner. As we sat together, her daughter, our granddaughter Clara, became a little fussy, which is not unusual for a baby only a few months old. My daughter, who has become a wonderful mother and a paragon of motherly wisdom, took little Clara and swaddled her in a warm blanket, snuggling her little arms and legs to the point where she could not move. I would have thought that such a "cocoon" would have been uncomfortable for Clara, but when Amy laid her down in her darkened bedroom, Clara stopped fussing and wiggling and simply fell asleep. Clara was snuggled in and safe in that warm blanket, as if she was experiencing a continuous, loving embrace in which there was only rest. Oh, that we would be similarly swaddled in God's embracing love, for this would truly quiet our souls.

One of the great texts of the Bible which describes this place of overshadowing in the Father's embracing love is Psalm 91:

*He who **dwells** in the **shelter** of the **Most High** will **abide** in the **shadow** of the **Almighty**. I will say to the LORD, "My refuge and my fortress, My God, in whom I trust!" For it is He who delivers you from the snare of the trapper And from the deadly pestilence. He will cover you with His pinions, And* *under His wings you may seek refuge; His faithfulness is a shield and bulwark* (Psalm 91:1-4, emphasis mine).

This Psalm is attributed by the old rabbis to Moses who spoke with the Lord "face-to-face" and who knew the presence of the Lord and His embracing love.[2] It is a portrait of life in the embrace of the Father, beneath the wings of the cherubim. The embracing love of the Father, as it is described in Psalm 91, is a place of "hiddeness" and refuge; overshadowing and abiding; rest and revelation.

"HIDDENESS" AND REFUGE

The embracing love of the Father is a place where we take shelter. The word for "sheltering," in Hebrew is *cether*, and it conveys the sense of hiding or concealing. It is a "secret place" (KJV) where one is alone with the Presence. "For in the day of trouble He will conceal me in His tabernacle; In the secret place of His tent He will hide me; He will lift me up on a rock" (Psalm 27:5).

The embracing love of God is not merely for the purpose of hiding from the consequences of sin; it is a "hiddeness" in the heart of God where we are no longer judged or assayed by human standards of appearance and righteousness. Mercy is a place of "refuge." (See Psalm 91:4.) The religious types of Jesus' day were always trying to find something wrong with Him, when all the while He was hidden in the heart of the Father. He was visible, yet not truly seen by them, as His life was lived within the embrace of His Father. (See Psalm 91:2-4; see also Psalm 36:7, 57:1-3.) We, who are hidden with Christ in God, are also seen but not known to the world. We live in the embrace of the Father and our lives are "hidden with Christ in God." (See Colossians 3:2-3.)

The embracing love of the Father is a place of belonging where we are simply those who are holy, chosen and beloved of God. (See Colossians 3:12.)

In the shelter of the Most High, we are hidden, just as when Moses entered into the glory cloud on Sinai. We are sequestered in God Most High, El Elyon, the One who sees from the highest place. We can therefore keep our focus on Him and He will see everything else. We move in His vision. We see life, ourselves, and everyone else as He sees.

In His embracing love we are in the shadow or under the covering of the Almighty, El Shaddai, the Most Powerful. Therefore, we can stop wiggling out of His embrace with each sin or failure by working in our own human strength. He supplies all the power to restore us. He brings us into this embracing love so that in Him we will live and move and exist. (See Acts 17:28.) Because of the Father's great tenderness toward us we live swaddled lives in His embracing love.

OVERSHADOWING AND ABIDING

Under the overshadowing wings of the cherubim is a place of darkness—overshadowing. This is not a formidable and fearful kind of darkness, but a quiet darkness where we are taken to the heart of the Father Himself. It is a place where all activity stops—where we stop moving. We no longer live in our own light, our own understanding and sense of righteousness. Under the overshadowing wings of His mercy we come to an awareness of the Father's beating heart and to a place of trust.

In 1977 I taught third grade for one semester at a Catholic school in western Pennsylvania. (It didn't take long to find out that these kids were too smart for me!) I cannot remember the names of the children now, except for one student who we will call Steven. Steven was one of those little boys who had something to say about everything. Most of what he offered walked a fine line between cute and annoying. But he always had something to say.

One day, as the school year was mercifully coming to an end, we took a couple of classes on a field trip to Laurel Caverns in western Pennsylvania. As we journeyed deeper into the caves, we reached a point where it was no longer possible to see any kind of natural light. At this point the tour guide offered to turn out the lighting system so that we could experience total darkness. As the lights went out, we were enveloped in the darkest dark I had ever experienced. I also experienced the very definition of the term "split second," because when the lights went out, Steven, our pint-sized commentator, grabbed onto and clung to my leg like a hound dog seizing a soup bone. The talking stopped and the clinging started in the darkness, as Steven reached out for something he could trust when he could no longer see. In the rest of that darkness there is One we can reach for—One we can always count on. We are not hidden from Him in the dark.

In the darkness we cling to the heart of the Father. David says, "In the shadow of Your wings I sing for joy. My soul clings to You; Your right hand upholds me" (Ps. 63:7-8). Under His covering wings of embracing love we can only sing and cling. God is not turning out the lights; He is bringing us into His embrace where we stop looking at others and stop criticizing ourselves and are joined to the heart of God as an unborn child and are aware of the beating of His heart.

REST AND REVELATION

Only when we are at rest, gathered to the heart of God under His wings, can we begin to see His heart and glory. Mercy is the glory of God. The dark rest that is experienced beneath the wings of the cherubim is at last the place of the embrace of the Father.

Mercy, the embracing love of God, is a place of safety and surrender that we enter by trusting in the heart of God. This embrace is the place of union with God and connection with His heart. It is the place of ultimate revelation of the heart of God where we are not so busy and distracted by trying to earn love and acceptance.

Beloved, we are safe under the covering wings of the cherubim as a place of refuge and intimate embrace. The mercy seat is the place where the deepest longing of God to be with us sequesters us with a love beyond reason. As we are safe and secreted against His breast, He brings us to a place of peace and unfolds His very heart to us. His heart is filled with *compassion*, bent toward us in *grace*, and expressed in *mercy. Mercy* is the intimate and embracing love of the Father.

ENDNOTES

1 Brennan Manning, *The Beloved* (Colorado Springs: NavPress), 59.
2 Ps. 91:1 The older Rabbis ascribed this psalm to Moses. Israel's exemption from the Egyptian plagues answers to the psalm. Thus it properly follows Moses' Ps. 90. (from Jamieson, Fausset, and Brown Commentary, Electronic Database. Copyright (c) 1997 by Biblesoft).

Turning Points

FEEL THE PASSION

Beloved, there is a place where the struggle ceases and union begins in the intimate embrace of the Father's heart. Allow the Lord to speak this place of rest as hiddeness to you, as you meditate on the following scripture. Read it to yourself aloud in a low tone until you can say it with your eyes closed.

> O LORD, *my heart is not proud, nor my eyes haughty; Nor do I involve myself in great matters, Or in things too difficult for me. Surely I have composed and quieted my soul; Like a weaned child rests against his mother* (Psalm 131: 1-3a).

Write down any words, thoughts, or images that occurred to you as you read this scripture.

What do these images or thoughts reveal to you about the heart of God?

Considering everything the Lord revealed to you through this scripture and the images and thoughts that followed. What is He speaking to you through your meditation? Record His personal word to you here.

EXPERIENCE THE PRESENCE

Beloved, there is a place where the struggle ceases and union begins in the intimate embrace of the Father's heart. So many distractions vie for our attention and steal the immediacy of relationship the Lord has for us. Allow yourself to get to a quiet place as you rest against the Lord's heart.

Listen carefully. Can you hear the beating of His heart as you come to rest against Him? Allow yourself to feel the warmth of the embrace. Allow yourself to hear the heart of God for you as He swaddles you in mercy, His embracing love. Chronicle your experience of resting against the Lord's breast here. Be sure to enter any additional thoughts or images the Lord brings to mind. Trust His breath in you.

SEE THE GLORY

Over the coming days keep a record of times when you feel the hovering wings of God's compassionate presence over you—when you sense the invitation to enter His quiet and secure embrace. List anything that keeps you from that embrace.

CHAPTER 13

The God of Tight Places

GOD IS OUR REFUGE AND STRENGTH,
A VERY PRESENT HELP IN TROUBLE (PSALM 46:1).

It was every parent's worst nightmare. I got the call as I was beginning a ministry session at about ten in the morning. I was told that our youngest daughter, Christina, who is better known as Coco, had been in an accident, but that she was okay. She had some kind of injury and was being taken to the local hospital emergency room.

I left the appointment with apologies and drove the short distance to the hospital where I was joined in a few minutes by my wife, Carol. She was the one who had been called first after the accident by someone at the scene. In fact our daughter herself had talked to her mother over the cell phone, though Coco was very confused about what had happened. Carol and I, like most parents, had to wait. It seems as though parents spend a large percentage of their time waiting.

We stood in the driveway of the emergency entrance, waiting for an ambulance to arrive, but it never arrived! We strained to see each time an ambulance arrived, always wondering if Coco was on board and expecting to hear her saying something like, "This is no big deal!"

119

Coco is our youngest—our baby. She is an impressive young woman with a desire to help and heal people in the community.

As we waited, it became apparent that Coco was not going to be coming there after all. We went inside the emergency waiting room and asked what they knew. All they could tell us was that they were not going to be receiving anyone from the accident, but that two of the three people had been life-flighted by helicopter to the trauma unit at the Hershey Medical Center and that one person had died at the scene of the accident.

The very words "trauma unit" shook us to the core. Our hearts fell and our pulse rates began to increase. By law the hospital personnel could give us no other information because Coco was over eighteen years of age. We were both frantic, and anger began to rise up in me. I began to insist that someone would give us some kind of information about our daughter's condition. Eventually I was given the number of the local state police station, and an understanding trooper told us that indeed Coco was one of those who had been airlifted to the trauma unit in Hershey.

We were given the number of the medical center in Hershey, and we called there. When we told them who we were, we were put on hold until our call was transferred to the hospital chaplain. He, like the others, was unable to tell us anything about Coco's condition other than the fact that he had talked to her and that the doctors were hard at work on her.

So Carol and I drove the one-and-a-half hour drive to Hershey, which seemed like about eight hours to us, for we were in a state of shock and total ignorance about our daughter's condition. I wish I could say that our hearts were encouraged by the fact that the Lord was in control and that everything would work out for good. However, I did not feel those assurances as we headed north on Interstate 81. I was afraid and could hardly hold myself together. As we drove to the hospital, many flashbacks replayed in my mind of times when our little one had been hurt or traumatized in various ways. I remembered when Coco was a newborn and they had to keep her in the hospital for an extra day because she was jaundiced. I remembered crying in the hallway when they told us. Then the scene jumped to when Coco was a toddler and fell against the hot glass window of an oven door. Her little hand and face were badly burned and became one giant blister. All she could do then was cry. I remembered other times when I felt helpless as a parent; the times when, as a father, I felt there was nothing I could do to help the "Bean," as we came to call her. But at no time in my life or hers did I feel as helpless and weak as I did on this day. My faith was wavering and my mind was wondering, "God, how could you allow this to happen to our baby? You gave her to us—why? How?

All of this was overwhelming to me and my impulse was to weep. But someone had to be the dad, and I figured it had to be me, though I felt more like a helpless, little boy than a father. All Carol and I could do was to pray, "Lord, have mercy on our daughter."

When we arrived at Hershey, we were taken to a little room adjacent to the trauma wing. In a few minutes a delightful man, Chaplain Herb, met us and prayed with us. He could not tell us anything about Coco but waited with us until one of the many doctors who were attending our "baby" could come and talk to us.

Eventually the doctor came in and began to describe what seemed like an incredible array of injuries that Coco had suffered. She had sustained far more than the few bumps and bruises we had expected at first. She had a broken pelvis, a dislocated hip, two broken feet, a deep laceration on her right knee, a fractured left wrist, and a long gash on her forehead, along with a broken cheekbone. This entire horrific inventory stunned us, but they were mere words to us at that moment.

After we heard the description of her injuries, we were told that we could see her in the Surgical Intensive Care Unit or SICU. We were taken to the unit and were greeted by the sights and sounds of medical high technology. The people were very friendly and accommodating. Coco's room was in the corner of the unit. We walked into the room through a sliding glass panel and caught sight of our daughter who was lying in a bed surrounded by lights and beeps and gauges indicating the various functions of her physical being. I walked around to the left side of the bed and caught sight of our bruised and bloody girl; she had a respirator tube down her throat, her hair was matted with blood, and there was a long, sutured cut on her pretty forehead. Then, as I looked at her, I spoke her name. "Coco," I said.

Her left eyelid rose, revealing one of those big brown eyes of hers. Though her body was battered, I knew there was still a Coco who was alive and unaltered in there somewhere.

At that point I did not know what to say to our baby. I knew she was experiencing pain beyond my imagination. Her little broken body lay helplessly on that sterile bed and there was nothing I could do about it. I wish I could say that the Spirit of God rose up in me and that I uttered great and faithful prayers. However, I could not pray; I was paralyzed and weak.

The mother of Coco's boyfriend came into the room and stood by her. She asked me, "Did you pray for Coco?" I could not even muster a response, as my eyes welled up with tears. I could not pray or say a word. All I could do was look at the various machinations of high-tech medicine and wonder to myself how we would be able to get through this challenging time. I was especially focused on myself, and I was feeling sorry and sad.

Coco had to go through something like sixteen hours of surgery over the next few days. We pretty much lived in the trauma center waiting room. I met a few interesting folk who were going through some of the same kinds of pain we were experiencing.

But everyone else seemed to have more faith than I did. I could not yet pray, as the breath had been knocked out of me. All the sermons I had preached on the goodness of God seemed to be only a memory in the far-distant past. This was my child! Where was the faithfulness of God now? Where was His protective hand? This wonderful young lady had pointed her life in the direction of helping others, and our family was dedicated to the Lord, and we had gone without so many things so many times for the sake of ministry. None of this was fair. None of it made sense. Where was the faithfulness of God?

A few days after the surgery, I felt that I needed to find closure, to make some kind of sense out of all that was happening to Coco and our family. We humans are always trying to make sense of things in order to gain some kind of control over our lives. I am convinced that all of us waste much energy trying to understand things that are not meant to be understood—to make sense out of the nonsensical.

The way I could get some closure was to go and see what was left of her car. I drove to the wrecking yard where they had towed the car after the accident, and I asked to see it. They knew immediately which one it was and led me to it. I saw only the back end of the car at first. When I came around to the front of the car I was amazed by what I saw. The front of her car and the passenger compartment were crushed and compressed into a tiny space. How could she have survived this impact? The airbag had been deployed, and it looked as if the steering wheel was bent over from the impact of her upper body. How did she not get crushed? As the fears of what might have been began to crowd into my mind, an odd peace began to settle within me. I heard God speaking these words to my heart: "I am abundantly available in tight places ..." It was an interpretation of Psalm 46:1 that I had preached on a few years before.

> *God is our refuge and strength, A very present help in trouble. Therefore we will not fear, though the earth should change And though the mountains slip into the heart of the sea; Though its waters roar and foam, Though the mountains quake at its swelling pride. ...The LORD of hosts is with us; The God of Jacob is our stronghold* (vs. 1, 7).

My interpretation of this scripture came from the notes in the margins of my Bible. According to the margin notes of the New American Standard Updated translation, the Hebrew of the text could be simply and literally interpreted as "God was abundantly available in tight places." I looked again at the car and saw that it was indeed a "tight place." God was telling me that He had been there in that "tight place" with Coco and in fact had been with her in every tight place she had ever experienced.

We have a tendency to see the presence of God as some kind of mysterious and impersonal force, like something out of Star Wars. But this was not some mysterious force that was with her, but the very person of Christ who was full of compassion for Coco.

As the Lord continued to speak to my heart, I could see Him in and around that crunched car in so many ways. I envisioned Him sitting beside Coco immediately before the crash and at the moment of impact. It was as though His hand had slipped between her and that airbag. Then I remembered that one of Coco's friends with whom she had gone through most of her junior high and high school years was driving by within a minute or so of the accident and saw the aftermath of the wreck. The Lord told her to pull over and help, as she had some medical training. She heard a voice from the car asking for someone to call Carol, her mother. Coco's friend stayed with her the whole time, praying with her and trying to stop the bleeding from an injury on her head. Her friend Larissa was the "present help, " the abundant availability of God, for that moment.

In addition to Larissa, a nurse who had been traveling behind Coco had a cell phone with which to call Carol. It was the comforting hand of God already beginning to assure us of His care, though at the time we did not hear Him through the din of trauma and worry. Next the scene switched to the EMT's on the scene. They were the hand of God all over Coco as she was flown to a place of help by the Life-line flight. It was a place that had been prepared by the love and compassion of God.

When Coco arrived at the trauma unit, as many as ten people worked on her at one time. There were plastic surgeons, neurosurgeons, orthopedic surgeons, and many other technicians. Though all of this looked like a high-tech medical wonder, it was in fact the "very present help" of God in that tight place. Chaplain Herb was the still, small voice of God speaking to us about our daughter. It was miraculous! It was the abundant availability of God on the scene.

The Lord had never taken His eyes off of Coco or withdrawn His hand from her. He reminded me that before Coco was ours, she was His. He reminded me of the other times when Coco or her sister, Amy Jo, had been injured or sick, the times when He was fully involved and abundant in those tight places. I began to see Coco's history and mine in a more accurate way. When she had to stay at the hospital after her birth, I now saw her cradled in the arms of one of the OB staff. (By the way, she was born at Hershey Medical Center as well.) When she was burned as a toddler, it was a kindly older doctor who ministered to her little face and hand so calmly and gently. On and on it went until I was finally able to see the Person of the Lord involved in every stage of her life and ours.

Many of us have accused God of apathy based solely on circumstantial evidence. We believe when we catch a cold or develop cancer that somehow God is disinterested in us, that He does not love us. We fail to see the faithfulness of God. The reality is that we live in a world that is filled with colds, cancers, and crashes as a result of the fall. These things are not God's fault, nor are they His will. They are just life.

The Lord is faithful to us in the midst of the inevitable trials we face. He did not tell us that we would never face trials, but that He we would be with us in trouble. He said, "... I will be with him in trouble; I will rescue him and honor him. With a long life I will satisfy him and let him see My salvation" (Ps. 91:15-16). To see His salvation is to see Him in the midst of the difficulty. The word salvation and the name of Jesus come from the same root. Jesus is the Person of God in the world of man. He is the fullness of God's mercy and faithfulness.

Again, God promised that He would be with us "in the fire." He promised:

> *"When you pass through the waters, I will be with you; And through the rivers, they will not overflow you. When you walk through the fire, you will not be scorched, Nor will the flame burn you. For I am the LORD your God ... "* (Isa. 43:2-3).

Coco is now married and a mother. Now, a few years after the accident, I was sitting at a local restaurant with Coco and her little girl, Hannah. I looked across the table at the face of my baby and noticed that there was a barely visible scar on her forehead. As I looked at this reminder of God's favor I was moved to tears (not a rare thing in my life these days). As we were leaving one another's company, I leaned over and kissed this little scar on her pretty forehead, though I did not make a big deal of it. This scar was a reminder of God's faithful and merciful intervention: the manifestation of His goodness to our family. I kiss the scars of Jesus' wounds as well as they too are reminders of His faithful intention and present love.

Now that I have seen the faithful hand of God at work in each of these circumstances, I am "... fully persuaded that, what he had promised, he was able also to perform" (Rom 4:21, KJV). God was never scared about what was happening to Coco in that accident; His heart did not go one beat faster through this. It was all in His hand, and Coco was hidden under His wings. And even if things had turned out far worse for us, even if Coco had been taken from us, we know that in some way it would have been His loving hand that led her to Himself. With Job, we would be able to say, "Though He slay me, yet will I trust Him!" (Job 13:15 NKJV).

The goodness and mercy of God do not rest upon our understanding or our faith, because my human faith and understanding are both puny weaklings. I cannot make sense of why something like this kind of pain should happen to Coco or to us. It does not make sense, but I am convinced that God planned to use this event for good. God's personal presence came to show mercy to our family, not because we deserved it but because He is good and His mercy is everlasting. He is "…abundantly available for help in tight places." The tighter the place, the more abundant He becomes. "Therefore we will not fear, though the earth should change And though the mountains slip into the heart of the sea …" (Ps. 46:2).

He is the God of tight places.

FEEL THE PASSION

We are surrounded by the benevolent presence and heart of the Father whose love is abundantly available to us. Meditate on the following scripture and allow the very present love of God to bring stillness to your heart through images, thoughts, and words that the Lord brings to you.

Cease striving and know that I am God (Ps. 46:10).

What kinds of words or images came to your heart as you meditated on this scripture? Describe them here.

What do these thoughts and images reveal about the heart of God and His present love?

Considering the scriptures and images that came to you, what is the Lord speaking to you personally about His present love toward you?

EXPERIENCE THE PRESENCE

We are surrounded by the present love of the Father. His love is abundantly available to us. Allow yourself to come to a quiet place in the presence of the Lord and ask Him to point out all the tight places in your life—places where you feel pressure. Maybe you are experiencing the pressure to perform or perhaps circumstances tightening around you. Remember, the tighter the place the more abundant is the presence and mercy of God.

Bring these tight places to the Lord and rest them in His presence. Experience the feeling of release as the Lord removes the pressures. Record the places in which the Lord brings His release.

SEE THE GLORY

In the days ahead, watch for the love of God to be manifested around you. Be aware of every invitation to become part of God's present and merciful love to those around you. Chronicle your observations and "God sightings" here.

CHAPTER 14

Touching the Father's Face

AND MOSES BESOUGHT THE LORD HIS GOD (EXOD. 32:11, KJV).[1]

And now, with the emblems of God's heart revealed to Moses over forty days and nights, a temporal disturbance came into the eternal presence. This Voice told Moses there was trouble in the camp, and commanded him to go down there at once. In their impatience and rebellion the people of God reduced the brilliance of the Incorruptible to the image of a slobbering, lumbering bull. "… They traded their glorious God for a statue of a grass-eating bull! They forgot God, their Savior, who had done such great things in Egypt …" (See Psalm 106:19-21, NLT.)

They tried to fashion the Eternal and Invisible God into something more visible and reasonable, a god that would go where they wanted to go. (See Rom. 1:22-23.) The righteousness and holiness of God was defiled, as His people defected from His embrace and turned to the empty and lifeless arms of a god they could *see*.

Now the awesome righteousness of heaven was aroused and God said, "Moses, get out of my way while I return this people to dust." But Moses, who had been immersed and saturated in the heart of

God for those forty days and nights, threw out his trembling hands to touch the face (the presence and heart) of God in a gesture of presentation. He began to present God's own heart back to Him again, saying, "These are *Your* people who have been delivered by *Your* hand and are living in *Your* promises. And it is *Your* heart that is on display to the world." Now, with His own heart reflected back to Him, the Lord breathed a deep sigh, resigning to His heart of compassion.

Moses' touching of the Eternal Face had not changed the heart of God, but it had revealed it! The Lord was within His right to erase the nation who carried His name, but He displayed His heart by calling them out of the camp of sin and to Himself. Those who responded were safe in the Eternal Hand; those who did not were consumed in their own callous rebellion. (Read the entire section of Exodus 32:9-14.)

TOUCHING THE FATHER'S FACE

Touching the Father's face is a humble presentation of desperate need, a gesture that releases the heart and character of God: mercy. Touching the Father's face is turning to something beyond our own heart and ability to do or to be—to the very character of God. Moses' entreaty went straight to the Fathering heart of God, where mercy was released to restore a fallen people, and this allowed them to come close to their Creator.

When we are in desperate need, we throw our arms out before the Father's face—our faces to His face. When I am in sin, I reach out to touch the Father's face and He forgives. When I need grace to forgive beyond my pain, I touch the Father's face and He allows me to see the offending person with the eyes of His heart and this releases him or her. As I touch the Father's face, He touches and transforms me, and His very heart is seen through me. As a case in point, I saw this transformational release in the passing of my father-in-law.

Carol's father, Raymond Mango, was confined to a bed in a nursing facility as he endured the final throes of pancreatic cancer. They were keeping him under heavy sedation due to the horrific pain that was caused by this rapidly advancing disease. During this dark time, he was usually unable to speak as he drifted in and out of consciousness.

One evening Carol and I were returning from a banquet when we were called by the nursing facility. As it turned out, it was Raymond himself who was on the phone. He had attained a little lucidity and was calling out for Carol. He wanted to see her. By the time we got to the home it was late at night. Carol's dad was lying asleep on the bed as we walked into his room. While he was still asleep, Carol leaned over her father, took his face in her hands and began to stroke it over and over again. She cupped her palms around his face, though his eyes were closed. He was weak and unable to do much more than receive her tender strokes of kindness.

She spoke softly, repeating, "Dad, I love you, I love you, I love you." As her hands gently passed over his face, he began to smile in response to her warm touch. Though he could not reciprocate, he clearly communicated that he was receiving what she was sending.

As I stood at the foot of her father's bed, I was in a state of wonder over the simplicity of the grace of God and how softly it flowed through Carol's hands. The child had become the parent at that moment simply because it was necessary and appropriate for that to happen. There was no loss of respect or honor—no absence of decorum. There was only love manifested in an act of mercy. Carol was touching her earthly father and her heavenly Father's face at the same time and the result was tender love.

In touching the Father's face we are transformed in His presence and we connect with who He is, and thereby we transmit His heart to the world. We are transformed just as Moses was transformed in the mountain of God for those forty days, and in that transformation the world is changed.

The Father brought His face near to us in the Son, Jesus Christ, Immanuel, who revealed the face of the Father to the world. Jesus was and is the truest representation of the Father's heart and glory in the earth. When we saw Him, we saw the Father, and what we saw in Jesus was the fullness of mercy and faithfulness. (See John 6:46 and 14:9.)

When we see Jesus, we see the genuine article—the Father's heart incarnate—the "... brightness of His glory and the express image of His person" (Heb. 1:3, NKJV).

THE "FALSE FACE" OF GOD

God was angry at the people of Israel because they had put a "false face" on Him. I believe the Lord was very angry with Israel over this apostasy for at least two reasons: first, in reducing God to a god they were misrepresenting His heart. "Thus they exchanged their glory For the image of an ox that eats grass" (Ps. 106:20).

God had warned His people about "graven images" or "false faces" that misrepresent Him in all His brilliance. "Then the LORD spoke to you from the midst of the fire; you heard the sound of words, but you saw no form—only a voice...So watch yourselves carefully, since you did not see any form on the day the LORD spoke to you at Horeb from the midst of the fire, so that you do not act corruptly and make a graven image for yourselves in the form of any figure ..." (Deut. 4:12, 15-16). Mercy is the glory of God, and that mercy is seen through men, as we touch His face and then the world.

The second reason for God's anger was that putting a "false face" on God took the focus of man away from the face of God. I wonder how much of the Father's face we truly see in our modern religion. Whether it is the detachment of formal religion, the structures of fundamentalism, or the emphasis on more fantastic and charismatic expressions, we paint a picture of the Father that is inaccurate. In so doing we put a "false face" on God whenever we do not act in accord with His character.

Now we have moved beyond the place for idle discussion and into the realm of manifestation. We need to be one mind with Christ! There is no evidence that Christ spent any time parsing the words of His Father. He simply *saw* and He was *moved* in obedience. His obedience was not obedience to a command or an edict but to the heart of the Father. The Son standing between heaven and earth saw our desperate need as we were captivated by sin and He turned to touch the Father's face to release the very heart and glory of God: mercy.

ENDNOTES

1 *besought*: In the original Hebrew this word literally meant to stroke the face of Jehovah for the purpose of appeasing His anger (i.e., to entreat His mercy, either by means of sacrifices or intercession).

Turning Points

FEEL THE PASSION

Beloved, we have a Father who has brought His face near to us to touch it. As we touch Him, He will transform us and the glory of God, which is His mercy, will be seen in the world. Meditate on the following scripture by speaking it aloud to yourself several times until you can say it with your eyes closed.

> *For though the LORD is exalted, Yet He regards the lowly ...*
> (Ps. 138:6).

Be sure to write down words, thoughts and images that came to you as you meditated on His word.

What do the thoughts and images that came to your mind reveal about the heart of God? Write your observations here.

Considering all that the Lord has shown you through His word and your observations, what is the Lord speaking to you personally? Write it here.

EXPERIENCE THE PRESENCE

Beloved, we have a Father who has brought His face near to us to touch it. Quiet your heart and fix the eyes of your heart on the throne of God. Experience the presence of the enthroned Lord as you place yourself in His presence and reach out to touch His face for the lost and wounded around you.

As you touch Him He will transform you, and the glory of God, which is His mercy, will be seen in the world. Write down the names of those for whom you are reaching out to touch the Father's face. Who are they? Family? Friends? Those who oppose or have wounded you?

SEE THE GLORY

Over the coming days be aware of the needs of people around you and reach out to touch the Father's face in prayer and intercession or acts of mercy. Journal about your intercession here.

PART THREE

Mercy

THE GLORY OF GOD

CHAPTER 15

"Show Me Your Glory!"

THEN MOSES SAID, 'I PRAY YOU, SHOW ME YOUR GLORY'
(EXOD. 33:18).

It is a pretty intimate request that Moses makes of the Sovereign of the universe, when he prays, "Lord, show me Your glory."[1] When we think of "glory," we may think of some great, brilliant display of power or some great accomplishment. God could have shown Moses any number of things. He could have shown him volcanoes or vast oceans on any other temporal display. But Moses was not asking for a fireworks display or some great feat of divine power. In effect Moses was saying to God, "Lord, show me what is the weightiest thing about you, the thing that distinguishes You above all others. Lord, show me your heart."

What is the glory of a person? Glory is what is precious and unique about an individual—it is how we *know* him or her. It is what reminds us of another as being a unique person. Occasionally when I travel and I'm going to be far from home, my wife, Carol, will spray a tiny bit of her perfume in my suitcase. She has worn that perform for a while and it has a distinguishing aroma that is something like cinnamon but sweeter. When I arrive at my hotel, I open my suitcase and before

I can do anything else, the fragrance of my dear wife pervades the room. It is as if she is there. When I smell her perfume, I can see her face and recall the sound of her voice in my heart. In every way that counts, she is with me. That aroma is like her glory, and it draws me back only to her.

The glory of God is what flows from the heart of God, and it is seen as our hearts become like His. If the glory of God is to be seen, we must become whatever God showed Moses when he said, "Lord, show me Your glory." The Voice must resonate in our hearts and transform us to become like Him.

THE GLORY OF GOD

What then was the glory that God showed to Moses? What was it that came flooding out concerning the heart of God? As Moses stood by, the Lord began to unfold His heart to him:

> *The LORD descended in the cloud and stood there with him as he called upon* **the name of the LORD**. *Then the LORD passed by in front of him and proclaimed, "The LORD, the LORD God,* **compassionate** *and* **gracious,** *slow to anger, and abounding in* **lovingkindness [mercy]** *and truth* (Exod. 34:5-6, emphasis mine).

The Lord descended and called out His goodness before Moses. His native goodness was on display, and in effect God said, "I am *compassion, grace,* and *mercy.*" Compassion is the *condition* of the Eternal Heart. Compassion is what fills the heart of God to the very deepest part. Grace is the out-flowing or *attitude* of His heart, and lovingkindness or mercy is the *expression* of His divine heart. Grace is love moving or extending toward the need. It flows like oil or the anointing of God.

God was saying to Moses and to us that the most distinguishing thing indigenous and unique to His heart is love expressed in *mercy* — the manifestation of the love of God. (See later chapters for more on compassion, grace, and mercy.)

The glory of God—the distinguishing and fragrant expression of His heart and character—is *mercy*. Mercy is the abounding weightiness of God's heart—the divine DNA, so to speak. Our healing, our anointing, our purpose, our ministry, and our destiny flow from the heart of God, which is extravagant with mercy and His passionate and present love.

God's glory does not come exclusively through greater spiritual manifestations, which our hearts crave in a purely carnal way. "The kingdom of God is not coming with signs to be observed; nor will they say, 'Look, here it is!' or, "There it is!' For behold, the kingdom of God is in your midst" (Luke 17:20-21). Mercy was right there in front of them in the Person of Jesus Christ, the fullness of mercy and faithfulness.

The glory of God, which *is* His mercy, will be *seen* as we live out the heart of God on the earth—as our hearts become healed and filled with *compassion*, bent toward others in *grace* and expressing the heart of a loving Father through *mercy*. God becomes *seen* as we cease reacting out of our own hurt and woundedness and begin responding to others out of the heart of God—when we stop trying to balance the scales with what is *fair* and instead do what *loves*.

This glory of the Lord is more than a fiery cloud; it is the consuming of our own fleshly nature as we turn toward the mercy of God. This glory tears down walls of hatred, overpowers pain, and overcomes evil with good. This glory feeds the hungry, clothes the naked, and brings prisoners out into the light of God's presence. This glory transforms mere men into harbingers of heaven. Compassion fills our hearts like oil fills a vessel or a jar. When our hearts are full compassion begins to overflow and spill out of the mouth and over the sides of the vessel and becomes grace. This grace flows until it encounters and object then begins to flow around and engulf that object or need. When the oil begins to flow around the object (i.e. someone with a need), it becomes an expression of mercy. Compassion fills, grace flows and mercy overwhelms.

The Torah and the Prophets tell us that the glory of the Lord will cover the earth; indeed, the earth will be filled with the knowledge of the glory of the Lord.

...but indeed, as I live, all the earth will be filled with the glory of the LORD (Num. 14:21).

"*For the earth will be filled With the knowledge of the glory of the LORD, As the waters cover the sea* (Hab. 2:14).

We, the beloved of God, minister His presence and heart when we respond in mercy. When we are turned toward mercy the glory of God is seen. We become like Jesus Christ—the fullness of God's mercy and faithfulness. (See John 1:14.) His glory becomes our glory.

Mercy is our manifest destiny in God. The glory of God will be *seen* on the earth, as the hearts of men begin to reveal the heart of a passionate and loving Father in the Earth. We will become "the fragrance of Christ." (See 2 Corinthians 2:15.)

Ernest Gordon was a prisoner of war in a hellish Japanese prison camp, which had a part in building the famous bridge over the River Kwai during World War II. He and a few others who were filled with the love of God discovered the essence of God's kingdom and glory there. As he recalled the work and heart of God that was stirring among the otherwise hopeless, Gordon writes, "We understood that the love expressed so supremely was God's love—the same love that we were experiencing for ourselves—the love that is passionate kindness, others-centered rather than self-centered, greater than all the law of men. It was the love that inspired St. Paul, once he had felt its power, to write, 'Love suffereth long and is kind [merciful].'" [2]

What Ernest Gordon and the others experienced and what flowed through them was mercy, the glory of God. That glory enabled them to love even their enemies in the face of cruel barbarism.

Beloved, if we are to see the Earth filled with the glory of God, it will happen through the sweet spikenard[3] flowing out of broken hearts who have taken their place at the feet of the Master and turned toward the mercy of God. And the house will be filled with the fragrance of that glorious love: His mercy.

THE UNFOLDING OF HIS GLORY

There is an unfolding throughout the scriptures that follows God's self-disclosure in Exodus 34:6. It goes from *compassion* to *grace* to *mercy*—the *condition*, the *attitude*, and the *expression* of God's heart of love. Some seek to find definition for each of these terms, but they are really just folds in the same garment of love that are unfurled over the need that is presented.

Throughout the gospels there is a pattern of Jesus "*seeing*," then being "*moved*" with compassion. When compassion arose, the anointing or grace arose, and then healing resulted. The order is compassion first, then grace/anointing, then mercy, or the expression of God's heart. "When He went ashore, He **saw** a large crowd, and **felt compassion** for them and **healed** their sick" (Matt. 14:14, emphasis mine). Jesus *felt* compassion, *went* ashore in grace, and *healed* to express mercy. He saw the need because He was looking. He was able to look beyond His own need and see the pain of the people around Him because He was focused on what the Father saw.

This all began because Jesus was utterly present to the needs of those around Him. This compassion then manifested the heart of the Father in healing or making a picnic for thousands of people out of a little boy's lunch.

The unfolding of God's glorious mercy was also seen in the story that Jesus told about the Samaritan man. When the religious types were trying to determine their legal obligation to love their neighbor, Jesus was revealing the mercy of God. He recounted that a Samaritan, who was on a journey, "… came upon him [the wounded man]; and when **he saw him**, he **felt compassion**, and **came to him** and **bandaged up his wounds**, pouring oil and wine on them; and he put him on his own beast, and brought him to an inn and took care of him" (Luke 10:33-34, emphasis mine).

The Samaritan man saw; then he was moved with *compassion*. He was not content to leave the wounded stranger alone to die when he had the power to help him. Then the Samaritan "came to him," got off his animal, and flowed toward the need of the wounded man.

This "coming to him" is the very picture of *grace*, where compassion flows down toward the need. When compassion disturbs the heart grace condescends to make the connection with the helpless and hopeless.

Finally, the Samaritan "bandaged his wounds," which was the expression of the *compassion* and the target of the *grace*. The unfolding was like this: compassion—the condition of the heart, then grace, which was the attitude of the heart, resulting in mercy, the expression of the heart.

And mercy does not end with a gesture; it is a faithful and committed love. The faithfulness of God is also reflected when the Samaritan man told the innkeeper he would pay whatever other expenses were necessary for this stranger he ministered to. In effect he took out his VISA card and said, "Put his care on my tab." God will not leave us alone until we get all the healing we are willing to receive.

A question and an observation came to my mind as I read the story Jesus told of the Samaritan man. Where did he get the cloth to bandage the wounded man? I doubt that he carried a first aid kit with him. No, he most likely had to dismember his own garment and use his own recourses of wine and oil to minister to the man.

This shows us that mercy costs us something whenever we extend it. Perhaps that is why there is so little of it. There is a price to be paid. The Father paid the total price by sending his only begotten Son, Jesus. The Son was torn from His side; the Trinity was dismembered in the same way that the Samaritan had to tear strips from his own garments to bring healing to this stranger.

There is an unfolding that must take place if we are to see the glory of God in the Earth. We must see what God sees, feel what He feels, love whom He loves, and heal what He heals. There is precious little real healing of people's hearts in the world today. We must see beyond ourselves and allow our hearts to be bent and to flow toward the needs we see. And, as the Father has done from the beginning, we must get our hands dirty.

A close friend of mine who is a college instructor in social work tells me there is only one gospel and it is inherently social. The gospel must be seen for it to be the Good News. The glory of God will be seen when we are focused on His heart, thereby allowing His love to flow through our hands.

ENDNOTES

1 In the Hebrew text the word "glory," *kabod* (the b is pronounced like a "v") refers to what is the most "weighty" thing or aspect.

2 Ernest Gordon, *To End All Wars* (Grand Rapids: Zondervan) 118.

3 John 12:3

Turning Points

FEEL THE PASSION

Beloved one, the Lord longs to unfold His glory to you, His passion for you, and His presence around you expressed in mercy—all so that His glory will cover your heart. Meditate on this verse by reading aloud to yourself in a low tone until you can say it with your eyes closed. Allow the Lord to speak His heart to you in words, thoughts, and images or any other way He desires.

> *Mary then took a pound of very costly perfume of pure nard, and anointed the feet of Jesus and wiped His feet with her hair; and the house was filled with the fragrance of the perfume* (John 12:3).

What kids of images and thoughts came to mind as you meditated on the scripture? Be sure to write down what the Lord shows you here.

What do the scriptures, words and images you have experienced here reveal about the heart of God? Record your revelations here.

What is the Lord now speaking to you personally concerning His glory? What do you see?

EXPERIENCE THE PRESENCE

Precious child of God, the Lord has invested much love in you to bring you to Himself. Allow the Father to hide you in the cleft of the rock as He did with Moses and then let Him unfold His heart to you. Feel His hand lifting you to a safe place in Him and then allow Him to point out to you the many times His glory, which is His mercy, has been seen in your life.

Write down what you sense the Lord unfolding to you as He unveils His glory before your eyes.

SEE THE GLORY

In the coming days keep a journal of places where you see the love of God demonstrated in mercy — where His heart is unfolded around you.

CHAPTER 16

Compassion: A Carrying Love

THE LORD DESCENDED IN THE CLOUD AND STOOD THERE WITH
HIM AS HE CALLED UPON THE NAME OF THE LORD. THEN THE
LORD PASSED BY IN FRONT OF HIM AND PROCLAIMED, "THE LORD,
THE LORD GOD, COMPASSIONATE" (EXODUS 34:5-6).

How many of us have ever been carried by someone when we were small children? There is a universal signal of a small child who wants or needs to be picked up and carried: two up-stretched arms aimed in the direction of the one whom the child selects for comfort, love, and holding. The resulting embrace releases healing, security, and love to the child.

I observed this signal recently at the Baltimore-Washington International Airport. I heard a little voice calling out, "Daddy! Daddy!" Then I turned to see a little girl running to her daddy with her arms up-stretched as she ran. Her father was getting off the airplane and she was there to greet him. It made me a little homesick, and I hadn't even left the airport yet. It made me think of my children and grandchildren who might have performed the universal "carry me" sign if they saw me under similar circumstances.

Being carried brings joy and comfort to the one who is carried and to the one who is doing the carrying. I have early and pleasant memories of being carried up to bed by my dad. He could carry both me and my twin brother at the same time. His carrying us gave us a feeling that we could never be dropped—that we would never fall. He carried us *surely*. He carried us because we were too little or too tired to make it up the stairs on our own.

Do you ever long to be carried? Do you ever become weary of carrying others who cannot carry themselves? *The calling of the body of Christ is to be carried and to carry those who cannot carry themselves.* We may well be the only arms available to them. Beloved, God loves us with a *carrying* kind of love. He longs to pick you up. He sees you and waits to see you give the universal sign that says, "Daddy, daddy, carry me."

When the Lord unfolded His heart before Moses, the first thing He called Himself was *compassionate*. Our English word *compassion* comes from the Latin word that literally means "to suffer with." God loves us with a carrying kind of love. So what is the Lord telling us about Himself when He tells us that His heart is one of compassion? He is telling us that He carries us when we cannot carry ourselves.

The Hebrew word translated as compassion in Exodus 34 comes from the same root as the word for the "womb."[1] When God was disclosing Himself to Moses, He was, in effect, telling Moses and us that He was carrying us in the womb of His own love. God describes His feelings for Israel in such intimate terms. Thus says Yahweh:

> *Is Ephraim [Israel] my dear son? My darling child?*
> *For the more I speak of him,*
> *the more I do remember him.*
> *Therefore my womb trembles for him;*
> ***I will truly show motherly compassion upon him.***[2]

God loves us with a carrying, suffering kind of love. So what is the Lord telling us about Himself when He tells us that his heart is one of compassion? He is telling us that He will carry us because we cannot carry ourselves. In effect, just as God said to Moses, He is saying to us that He is carrying us in the womb of His own love.

The womb is a place of intimate awareness where all the resources of the mother are focused on sustaining the child who is being carried in the most secure and intimate place. The womb of God's love is an even more secure location:

> *"Can a woman forget her nursing child And have no compassion on the son of her womb? Even these may forget, but I will not forget you"* (Isa. 49:15).

Compassion is what our heart *feels* in the presence of need just as a mother is moved or disturbed by the need of the child she carries. Compassion arises as the one who carries is utterly present to the one being carried.

CARRYING THE ONE WHO CARRIED ME

About a year before my father passed away, I traveled to western Pennsylvania to stay at my parents' home for a few days while my mother was in the hospital. My mother was in the hospital and my father was going through the final throes of Alzheimer's. I was looking forward to spending a couple of days with my sister Carol who had been carrying most of the load for our parents in their later years.

When I got to my parents' home, Dad greeted me at the kitchen door with his usual smile. All seemed to be well at that moment. We sat down and had some lunch together and to my surprise Dad asked me whether or not I was married. Of course I said I was. Then Dad asked if I had any children. Somewhat surprised and unsettled by this question, I took out my wallet and showed him some pictures of my children. He seemed satisfied for the moment and lunch continued. About ten minutes later, Dad looked at me again and asked, "So, are you married?" My heart sank as reality began to dawn on me that Dad had no recollection of our conversation that had taken place just a few minutes before. So once again I took out my wallet and showed Dad the pictures. This sequence was repeated a few times until it was time to go to the hospital to visit my mother.

We made the short drive to the hospital to visit Mom, and we enjoyed sightseeing along the way. Dad was pleased to see Mom, though he was a little confused as to why she was in the hospital. On the drive home from the hospital, we passed by a large church where I had played in several trumpet recitals and performances years before. My dad had attended nearly every concert or recital in which I had ever performed. He even showed up in some pretty crummy places where I played with a combo. But when I asked him, "Do you remember coming to hear me play at that church, Dad?" he said, "Play what?"

I felt as though I was sitting in the car with a stranger. "Trumpet, Dad. I played the trumpet."

"No, I can't say I remember anything about that. It's a pretty church though."

We returned to Dad's house and sat down in the TV room. I didn't quite know what to say or how to respond to him. What could we talk about? What would he remember? Dad sat in front of the TV with a glazed look on his face watching something I knew he would forget before the next commercial. As I observed this man who had held the family together, the one who had carried me to bed as a baby, my focus began to change and I was beginning to *see* the need.

Once I got my attention off myself, I asked, "Dad what do you want to do right now?

He said, "It's a nice day. I'd like to go for a walk up the road." So we put on our jackets and took a walk up the road for a half mile or so and back again. The whole time Dad talked about the cows in the field or the weather or whatever came into our field of vision. When we got back to the house, we sat down at the table for a minute and had something to drink.

Then I asked, "Dad, what would you like to do now?"

He said, "Well, it's a pretty day. Why don't we go for a walk?"

Rather than tell him we had just gotten back from a walk, we took another walk. We retraced our steps of only a short time before, but I didn't mind. At some point this visit had ceased to be about me. It was all about what Dad needed and wanted at the moment.

When we returned from our second walk, supper time was approaching. I asked, "Dad, what are you hungry for? What would you like to eat?"

He wasted no time in answering me. "Ice cream!" There was no doubt in his mind what he wanted, so we got in the car and went to the local Dairy Queen where we both got large, hot fudge sundaes. As we sat at the DQ, we traded no deep thoughts; we just discussed the way the ice cream and hot fudge tasted. This was Dad's time. Dad, who had taught me many things over the years—everything from tying my shoes to catching a baseball to living with integrity— was teaching me another valuable lesson, this time on *compassion*. He was teaching me to carry the one who had carried me so many times before.

I learned to minister in the present tense during that visit in which nothing was important except Dad. I miss Dad even now, and it's been several years since his passing. But I know that he is in the presence of One who is pure compassion and is enjoying something far better than hot fudge.

Compassion did not fill or move my heart until I turned away from myself and toward Dad; then I was able to be utterly present to the needs of my dad. I had to be able to *see* Dad and his needs in order for compassion to well up in my heart. *Seeing* is the key.

SURELY HE CARRIES OUR SORROWS

We have a Father who carries us securely in His heart. He carries and has always carried us as a father carries his child, because we are too little to carry ourselves.

> "... the LORD your God carried you, just as a man carries his son, in all the way which you have walked until you came to this place" (Deut 1:31).

Like a shepherd, He carries us securely to safety and to pasture. A shepherd gathers his lambs—the young ones who lack ability to get safely to places of feeding. He carries them because if He didn't, they would be at the mercy of wolves and jackals.

> Like a shepherd He will tend His flock, In His arm He will gather the lambs and carry them in His bosom; He will gently lead the nursing ewes (Isaiah 40:11).

The Father has always carried us and is committed to never put us down. He says,

> *Listen to Me, O house of Jacob, And all the remnant of the house of Israel, You who have been borne by Me from birth And have been carried from the womb; Even to your old age I will be the same, And even to your graying years **I will bear you! I have done it, and I will carry you; And I will bear you and I will deliver you*** (Isaiah 46:3-4, emphasis mine).

When He says, "I will be the same," He is literally saying in the Hebrew, "I carry you because I am He!" He carries us because that is who He is: a carrying, loving Father. He carries all who will be carried—all who lift their arms and declare they are too little or too weak to carry themselves.

Jesus was the greatest expression of the compassion that so fills the Father's heart. He loves with that carrying kind of love. The Gospel of Mathew tells us:

> *"Jesus was going through all the cities and villages, teaching in their synagogues and proclaiming the gospel of the kingdom, and healing every kind of disease and every kind of sickness. **Seeing** the people, He **felt compassion** for them, because they were distressed and dispirited like sheep without a shepherd"* (Matt. 9:35-36, emphasis mine).

The prophet Isaiah speaks of the coming Messiah's carrying love when He says, "Surely our griefs He Himself bore, And our sorrows He carried" (Isa. 53:4). The many times I have read these words, I have seen Jesus loaded down with my sin and sorrows on His back. I suppose that is the best sense of Isaiah's words, but I wonder if we might dare to paint an even more intimate picture.

I see a different and more intimate picture now as I read these words. I see that Jesus was a man who was "… despised and forsaken of men, A man of sorrows and acquainted with grief …" (Isa. 53:3). I see that He was a man who understood something about pain of all kinds. It is more than a comfort to me when I am in physical or emotional pain, to know there is One who is carrying the same pain I am carrying and to know that my pain disturbs the living God as He carries me in this most intimate love.

Jesus, who enjoyed the most intimate of relationships with the Father's heart, *saw* what the Father saw and *felt* what was in the Father's heart. Jesus said, "Truly, truly, I say to you, the Son can do nothing of Himself, unless it is something He sees the Father doing" (John 5:19). When Jesus healed someone, he was responding to the heart of the Father.

Compassion *sees* the need and stirs the heart. If the needy one is stuck in sin, then the Father's heart is filled with compassion and manifests mercy in forgiveness. If the needy one is wounded, then the Father's heart is filled with compassion and disturbed within Him to such an extent that He sends healing. If the needy one is ignorant of the Father's heart, then compassion is manifested as teaching. The Father's heart is "filled with compassion" and He releases it to our benefit. (See Psalm 78:38, Psalm 86:15, Psalm 111:4, Psalm 112:4, and Psalm 145:8.)

We humans are puny when it comes to having compassion on our own, because we are usually insecure and focused on ourselves rather than seeing the need around us. As we grow in our awareness of the intimate security that is found in the womb of God's love, we can begin to carry others. It is the heart that is intimately connected with God that sees what the Father is doing and then does the same.

If we live in ignorance of the naked and wounded around us, we need to reconnect to the heart of God. "But whoso hath this world's good, and seeth his brother have need, and shutteth up his bowels of compassion from him, how dwelleth the love of God in him?" (1 John 3:17, KJV).

Compassion is the seed of His life planted within us that grows and fills our hearts; it displaces everything else in order to see the need. As with any seed, there must come a death before there can be life. Jesus said that a grain of wheat has to die before it can bear fruit. (See John 12:24.) There must be an emptying before there can be a filling. The question is: what seeds are we carrying in our hearts?

Paul tells us that compassion has to be the condition of our hearts as we live with one another. He says, "So, as those who have been chosen of God, holy and beloved, put on a heart of compassion, kindness, humility, gentleness and patience; bearing with one another, and forgiving each other, whoever has a complaint against anyone; just as the Lord forgave you, so also should you" (Col. 3:12-13).

Compassion is the condition of the Father's heart that flows to us as life would flow to the unborn in the womb. We become as the One who carries us. When the seed of compassion has germinated, it cannot remain inert, and it wells up to become *grace*.

Whatever it is that you are carrying, remember, you are not carrying it alone. He is at this moment carrying the pain you carry. Because He is eternal, He began to carry our pains long ago. Christ saw us from the cross.

There is a story from the United Kingdom about a businessman who went home at the end of long day and was greeted at the door by his little girl who was in a wheelchair. The little girl greeted her father with a smile and said, "I can carry your briefcase upstairs if you like."

The father smiled but said, "Sweetheart, you can't carry my briefcase up the stairs in your wheelchair."

She replied, "Daddy, I can carry anything if you carry me."

Whatever we carry, He is carrying us in a secure, loving way, and He will not put us aside or call a babysitter to take care of us. We are safe in His compassionate love. Will you lift your arms to Him and say, "Abba, carry me"? We enter into a secret place of rest when we are hidden in the womb of God's love.

ENDNOTES

1 OT:7355 racham (raw-kham'); a primitive root; to fondle; by implication, to love, especially to be compassionate: KJV - have compassion (on, upon), love, (find, have, obtain, shew) mercy (-iful, on, upon), (have) pity... (Biblesoft's New Exhaustive Strong's Numbers and Concordance with Expanded Greek-Hebrew Dictionary. Copyright (c) 1994, Biblesoft and International Bible Translators, Inc.)

2 Jeremiah 31:20 Interpretive translation of Jeremiah 31:20 Phyliis Trible, *God and the Rhetoric of Sexuality* (Philadelphia: Fortress, 1978), pp. 43-45, 53.

Turning Points

FEEL THE PASSION

Precious one, you are safe in the womb of the Father's love even as you read these words. Grow in that safety now, as you meditate on His Word. Read the scripture to yourself until you can say it with your eyes closed. Allow the Lord to speak His love to your heart through thoughts, words, and images.

> In all their affliction He was afflicted, And the angel of His presence saved them; In His love and in His mercy He redeemed them, And He lifted them and carried them all the days of old (Isaiah 63:9).

What kinds of thoughts or images came to mind as you meditated on the scripture? Write them down here.

What do these words and images reveal to you about the heart of God who has carried you in His tender mercies?

Considering all the Lord has revealed to you in the scripture, what is He speaking to you personally? Write His personal communication to you here.

EXPERIENCE THE PRESENCE

Beloved, we have a Father who carries us deep in His heart. When we hurt, He hurts. The Lord feels grief for us even as He carries us in the womb of His love. Let us enter into the womb of the Father's love for us. Allow yourself to come to a place of stillness in His presence and begin to feel the surrounding security of His carrying love. This is a place where once again we come to hear His heart. But also be assured that He hears ours as well.

Describe what it feels like to be safe and secreted away with the Lord—to know that He hears your heart and carries your sorrow. Ask the Lord to bring to mind anything you feel like carrying alone and let Him carry you as you carry whatever He has revealed. Maybe you have carried a sickness or a wound or a worry. Let Him carry you now. Write your thoughts on His carrying love here.

SEE THE GLORY

Keep a journal over the coming days when you become aware of the Lord carrying you in His great and tender love for you. These are places to remind yourself that you are being carried and that you are not in your life alone.

CHAPTER 17

Grace: A Love that Reaches Down

THE LORD, THE LORD GOD, COMPASSIONATE AND GRACIOUS
(EXOD. 34:6, EMPHASIS MINE).

One morning in a healing prayer session, a young man who had been at one of our recent seminars described a picture the Lord had given to him. This young man had grown up in the Middle East where he was part of a large family. When he was a little boy, his family would travel to apple orchards in Syria where each of the children would be given a little basket to gather apples from the trees.

My friend, let's call him Hakim, was the smallest of the children and was not able to reach even the lowest branches of the apple trees that were laden with fruit. They were just out of his reach. The other children made fun of the little boy, who tried to stretch his arm and jump as high as he could to reach just one apple. But his every attempt was to no avail. He was just too small.

Hakim has grown into a large man, who is smart and strong, but occasionally he still feels like the little boy who was too short, the boy to whom all of life seemed out of reach. The apples seemed to always exceed his reach. Finally the little boy settled for the bruised and rotting apples he could find on the ground, the apples that had fallen off the tree. His life had often become one of settling for what was laying about, believing that he was destined for something less rather than something great.

When the young man was at our seminar, he received a vision of the little boy as we prayed for the Lord to reveal areas of wounding and limitation in our lives and to show us where they originated. The second part of the prayer was that the Lord would express His presence and reveal truth to us in our places of wounding. It was in this second part of the prayer that the Lord gave him a beautiful illustration of grace, which the young man described during his appointment. As the child reached toward the illusive and unobtainable fruit, the Lord simply released it from the tree and it fell right into little Hakim's basket. God had done what the little boy could not. The Lord told the child that He saw and was moved by his pain and He felt compassion for him. He released the apple to him simply because He loved him, and He wanted Hakim to know that he no longer had to settle for what was rotten and laying around on the ground.

What a picture of grace this is. *Grace is the love of God that reaches down to provide what is out of our reach.* While compassion fills and moves the heart, grace is love that becomes restless and bends to respond to the need. Grace is the hand of Jesus that reached out to Peter to keep him from going beneath the waves simply because Peter reached out in dire need and trust to Jesus. (See Matthew 14:26-31.)

The word *grace* is translated from the Hebrew word *chanan*, which literally means "to lean or to be bent toward something." In grace there is an inclination. The Psalm says, "I waited patiently for the LORD; And He inclined to me, and heard my cry" (Ps. 40:1, NKJV, emphasis mine). Another Psalm declares, "Because He has inclined His ear to me, therefore I will call upon Him as long as I live" (Ps. 116:2, NKJV).

Grace is an attitude or an inclination toward the helpless and the humble. It's important to remember that God's plan always involves law to the proud and grace to the humble.

Though grace is a broad term with many theological shades, we are going to talk only about grace as an attribute of the heart of God.

Grace is the liquefying of the compassion within the Father's heart. Jesus and grace are all about the availability of the love of God. The same pattern we see in Exodus 34:6, which unfolds the glory of God, applies to the Father sending the Son:

> *For God **so loved** the world that He **gave** His only begotten Son, that whoever believes in Him should not perish but have everlasting life* (John 3:16, NKJV, emphasis mine).

God loved (this is His compassion), God gave/sent His Son (this is His grace), and Jesus died (this is His mercy). Jesus is the personification, the very incarnation of the grace of God. He left or emptied His throne and took the form of a bond servant, the lowest of all levels. Love had to flow all the way down in order to bring us all the way back up to the Father. (See Philippians 2:7.)

People, especially Christians, seem to always be looking to find the line between grace and foolishness. They don't want to be "suckers," and they want to know how far they have to extend love. The answer, as far as I can see in the Scriptures and the heart of God, is that we must go as far as we need to go when and if there is a response.

Consider the Parable of the Prodigal Son:

> *And He said, "A man had two sons. The younger of them said to his father, 'Father, give me the share of the estate that falls to me.' So he divided his wealth between them. And not many days later, the younger son gathered everything together and went on a journey into a distant country, and there he squandered his estate with loose living. Now when he had spent everything, a severe famine occurred in that country, and he began to be impoverished. So he went and hired himself out to one of the citizens of that country, and he sent him into his fields to feed swine. And he would have gladly filled his stomach with the pods that the swine were eating, and no one was giving anything to him. But when he came to his senses, he said, 'How many of my father's hired men have more than enough bread, but I am dying here with hunger! I will get up and go to my*

*father, and will say to him, "Father, I have sinned against heaven, and in your sight; I am no longer worthy to be called your son; make me as one of your hired men."' So he got up and came to his father. But while he was still a long way off, his father **saw him and felt compassion** for him, and **ran and embraced him and kissed him"** (Luke 15:11-20, emphasis mine).*

This prodigal son was someone's baby boy—their precious child. He, no doubt, was the object of the hopes and affections of his parents for many years before he left town. Somewhere along the line, this child left his father's embrace and wanted all he could get from his dad in order to meet some kind of addictive need within him. This was a need his father would have been all too eager to meet, perhaps, if the boy had only turned to him.

This son ended up in the pigpen, about as far in every way as he could be from his father and his culture. What was a nice Jewish boy like him doing in a place like that? The son had to come to the end of his own resources in order to reach out to his father. That is the problem with all of us in that we are separated from the Father's embrace because we are still trying to handle things our own way, in our own strength. This boy's pockets and his heart were empty, and then he remembered the heart of his father. The text says, "He came to his senses." A better and more literal rendition might be that he "came to himself."[1] He began to remember that he was a son. In that remembering he humbled himself by saying that he was no longer worthy to be a son, but would be a servant.

A river of grace was about to be released. This son had turned away from his father, and in his remembering he was now about to turn and face Dad. That remembering was an invitation back into the father's embrace. Note that until this child turned, the father had to stand at the gate, watching and heartbroken. He could not send the rent money to the pigpen, because that would sustain the son in a lost condition, and he would be separated from his father's embrace. He loved him enough to be patient.

I have met many times with weeping and frustrated parents whose children have fallen into drugs and bad times. They have in some cases enabled their children to continue in their way by supporting and providing for them with no repentance. They believed this to be merciful but, in fact, it is just the opposite. They are concerned more about their own pain or image than what is good for their child. Every time they pay a bill or bail them out, they are "sending a rent check to the pigpen." Some may call a parent's unwillingness to help a child out of a similar situation "tough love," but in reality is it love in is purest form, because it allows the child to get out of the pigpen and to be pointed back to God.

The Father has stretched His arms out to us, but we must turn and accept His embrace. Listen to the plaintive cry of the Father's heart: "I have spread out My hands all day long to a rebellious people, Who walk in the way which is not good, following their own thoughts" (Isa. 65:2). In this passage you can hear the anguish of the Father who stretches His fingers out as far as possible, but He feels strained and aching with His longing to embrace His beloved children. However, He will not grab us by the scruff of the neck and command us to receive His favor. The father of the prodigal son loved his boy, but he was stuck at the gate until his son would choose to turn back to him again.

Grace is not automatic, for it requires acceptance. Grace is an invitation, but unless we respond affirmatively to the invitation, no one will come and drag us to the table. First, we must accept the invitation. Listen to the promises of scripture to all those who remember their Father and turn around to Him:

> For if you return to the LORD, your brothers and your sons will find compassion before those who led them captive and will return to this land. For the LORD your God is gracious and compassionate, and **will not turn His face away** from you if you return to Him (2 Chronicles 30:9, emphasis mine).

> **They refused to listen, And did not remember** Your wondrous deeds which You had performed among them; So they **became stubborn** and appointed a leader to return to their slavery in Egypt. But You are a God of forgiveness, Gracious and compassionate, Slow to anger and abounding in

lovingkindness; And You did not forsake them. (Nehemiah 9:17, emphasis mine)

But You, O Lord, are a God merciful and gracious, Slow to anger and abundant in lovingkindness and truth. **Turn to me, and be gracious to me;** *Oh grant Your strength to Your servant, And save the son of Your handmaid* (Psalm 86:15-16, emphasis mine).

And rend your heart and not your garments. Now **return to the LORD your God, For He is gracious** *and compassionate, Slow to anger, abounding in lovingkindness And relenting of evil* (Joel 2:13, emphasis mine).

Grace is not released until it is needed or requested. Grace, even for salvation, is not released as long as we try to do it ourselves. Self-effort is a dam that shuts up the gracious flow of the Father's love.

Note what happens when the son turns and begins to move back toward the father. This story unfolds the glory of the Father in the same way Moses experienced it in Exodus. *"But while he was still a long way off, his father* **saw him and felt compassion** *for him, and* **ran and embraced him and kissed him."**

The child had not gotten out of hell's driveway and the father *saw* him. This seeing stirred the father's *compassion*. He was no longer stuck at the gate. This father longs, as our Father longs, to pour out grace. The prophet says, "Therefore the LORD longs to be gracious to you, and therefore He waits on high to have compassion on you" (Isa. 30:18). In this verse I see the image of a Father who, seeing us at our worst and most helpless, experiences a broken heart for His children who are separated from His embrace.

With His compassion aroused and seeing now the son's face, the father was released from the gate, and he ran to meet his son along the way. This was *grace*, the reaching-down love of God in its fullest flower. The Father seems to be more interested in direction than perfection.

When I was young man in college and had no relationship with the Lord, I was playing in a band that occasionally played in places where you would not want to take your mother. My dad showed up in many places where I played through the years, but mostly he came to the more formal, legitimate kinds of gigs.

One night, however, I was playing in a local bar—one of those less formal places. Somewhere around the end of the second of four sets, I looked up and saw my dad walking across the back of that joint in the gloom of cigarette smoke and the aroma of beer. He walked to one of the back tables and sat down to listen to his son play music. I could see the embers and smoke of his corncob pipe as he sat and listened to me play. He never said a word to me, only listened until the end of the set when he said something like, "Sounded good." That is a picture of grace—a grace that came where I was. I will never forget that night. You see, grace consumes distance.

I wonder what was in the heart of the prodigal son as he saw his dad scandalously running to meet him with tears streaming down his face. Did the son ache as much for the embrace as the father ached to embrace him?

When the distance between them had been totally consumed by the father's grace, the son put his head upon the breast of the father and the father wrapped himself around the son to kiss and embrace him. Note that he kissed the son. That is the Father's heart. We were created face-to-face to live face-to-face with the Father. This father of the prodigal son kissed his boy alive again with his own breath, then he swaddled him in a tender embrace. This was the expression of *compassion* and destination of *grace* in the act of *mercy*.

There is a river of grace that waits to be released so we will return to the Father's presence and embrace. There was an amazing scene in the movie *Lord of the Rings, The Two Towers*. The battle between the armies of man and the evil Orks was beginning to turn in favor of the armies of man. There was a group of giant, walking trees who had joined the fight against the Orks. They were closing in on *Eisengard*, the subterranean domain of the evil *Salron*. There was a large dam that had been constructed to hold back the river, leaving the landscape dry and barren.

As the battle advanced upon the very gates of evil, Treebeard, the leader of the giant, walking trees, said, *"Release the river!"* Upon that command the dam broke and a torrent of water was released, crashing over the dry landscape and washing away the forces of evil while dismantling the infrastructure of hell.

The release of that river is much like the grace that is released to destroy the forces of hell and darkness at work in the world.

There is a river of grace that is released as we turn toward the Father, and it is released every time we turn toward Him. To be sure, we will turn away occasionally. But when we do, He is waiting heartbroken at the gate to see our faces and run to meet us.

ENDNOTES

1 From the Greek word *heautou*, a reflective pronoun, i.e. "himself."

Turning Points

FEEL THE PASSION

Priceless one, grace awaits you. It is the reaching-down love of the Father that is released every time you turn toward Him. Meditate on the following scripture and allow yourself to hear the Father's heart for yourself. Read it to yourself several times aloud until you can say it with your eyes closed. Be aware of any thoughts, words, or images that come to your mind as the Father speaks to your heart. He longs to be gracious to you.

> *Behold, as the eyes of servants look to the hand of their master...So our eyes look to the LORD our God, Until He is gracious to us* (Ps. 123:2).

Write down anything you sense the Lord speaking to you as you meditate upon this Scripture.

What do the words and images you received in meditation reveal about the Lord? Write your comments here.

What is the Lord speaking to you personally through the words and images you received? Put yourself in the picture and make His word personal.

EXPERIENCE THE PRESENCE

Chosen one, the Lord has an apple for you today. Put yourself in a safe place with the Lord—maybe that apple orchard that Hakim talked about at the beginning of the chapter. Allow yourself to see and sense His presence. What are the apples that seem to be out of reach to you? Where have you settled for the bruised fruit lying around?

Stretch out your hand and allow the Lord to drop that apple in your basket. Maybe it's an apple of understanding or forgiveness for you or someone else. Receive it now. Be sure to write down anything the Lord releases to you as you stretch out your arms to Him.

SEE THE GLORY

Be watchful over the coming days to see where the Lord drops other apples in your basket. What seems out of reach to you? Watch now how the Lord stretches toward you releasing grace, the love that reaches down.

CHAPTER 18

Mercy: The Weight of Glory

I sat with a man one morning whose wife was living in an adulterous relationship. To make matters worse, everybody in his church knew about it. He not only felt crushed, but he felt exposed and embarrassed, as well. He was reaching out for any kind of help he could get. As we sat together, we probably wept as much as we prayed together.

The thing that struck me was the incredible weight of pain that this man was carrying. It was a heavy weight of unfairness. This man had done all he could do, and his wife still made a deliberate choice to betray her marriage and her family. I remember how this young man lowered his head and sobbed, because it all seemed hopeless in the natural. He was confronted by a basic decision to either cut her loose or to wait for her.

As we prayed together, the Lord gave him the grace to make a decision to wait for his wife. Her behavior was beyond all reasonable bounds, and it required an unreasonable love for him to do this. Mercy was the only thing that could possibly bring her to her senses. This brother had come to the deliberate decision that he was going to allow love to outweigh the embarrassment and offense he was experiencing.

After some period of time, the wife did return to her family and they began anew. This was possible only because he chose a higher righteousness and because "Mercy triumphs over judgment" (James 2:13, NKJV).

What would the world say of this kind of love? Most reasonable folk, even some professing Christians, would say the man had a right to cut his wife loose and let her go. He would be a fool to do anything else. But he chose to love beyond all reasonable bounds and to own his part in their troubled marriage. He chose to allow the love of God to outweigh his hurt, and the glory went to God. Mercy was the weight of God's glory, which outweighed the hurt and restored a family.

Beloved, it is not a matter of *if* we will encounter unfairness and personal hurt, but *when*. However, like the man and his wife who struggled in their marriage, we always have a choice to make and it is not necessarily going to be a rational one. We, too, will be presented with a choice of either law or love.

THE SCALES OF JUSTICE

Each of us has something like a justice system in our hearts that resembles those ancient scales that are depicted with two bowls suspended from a straight arm. Weights were placed on one side of the scale; then an equal weight needed to be placed on the other side of the scale until the top beam of the scale straightened out.

You and I are always trying to figure out what is fair—what balances the scale, so to speak. Somebody hurts us and we place a weight on the scale against them. Perhaps someone betrays us and we hold onto that betrayal as if it were money. Reality says that we live most of our lives in almost every realm with an unbalanced scale, whether in the church, in our marriages, or in any other kind of relationship.

We even weigh the scales concerning ourselves, wondering whether we are worthy or less worthy, and basing our worthiness on our ability to live according to our understanding of perfection. When we find something we believe to be unworthy about us, or perhaps even a sin, we look for ways to throw some kind of weight on the other end of the scale to balance things out. This, in fact, is the essence of religion, religion that separates us from the presence of God. It is hopeless—even breathless—because we will never be able to find enough good works or weights to put on the scales opposite our sin. We are stuck, and we are unable to see anything but the scale.

In the shortest of the New Testament parables Jesus said, "...a blind man cannot guide a blind man, can he? Will they not both fall into a pit?" (Luke 6:39). Jesus paints a picture of the Old Covenant in which the economy was based on "an eye for and eye." This scale of justice in our hearts would have us extract an eye for each offense that is committed against us. Gandhi said, "An eye for an eye makes the whole world blind." Jesus is saying that we cannot poke out enough eyes to make things fair and that there has to be another way. If we live under the rule of this law, we will all end up blind and in the pit.

Jesus is talking about a balancing act we may try to live out, one in which we try to get the crossbar on the top to be level somehow. Each of us drags bags of weights around, trying to outweigh the offenses that are committed against us or the offenses we have committed against somebody else or God. Someone hurts me and a weight goes into the bag. I extend grace to someone by going to the back of the line, and by doing so a weight goes in the bag to outweigh some future imbalance. This weight is killing us and taxing our hearts.

This scenario reminds me of *The Mission*. A conquistador (played by Robert De Niro) killed somebody and then was sentenced to carry his armor and weapons around as a penance. Finally, this soldier came to a place where he was no longer able to carry the weight, and suddenly someone cut the rope that bound the weight to him, and the armor went splashing into the river below.

I wonder whose armor we are carrying around that restricts and compromises our relationship with the Father. What kinds of weights have I placed around the necks of other folk with whom I disagree or those who may have wounded me in the past? The carnal truth is that it feels good and righteous to carry around that bag of weights, but it taxes my heart and robs me of intimacy. And in the end it kills my spirit. (See 2 Corinthians 3:6.)

Jesus says, "Do not judge so that you will not be judged. For in the way you judge, you will be judged; and by your standard of measure, it will be measured to you" (Matt. 7:1). Whatever weights we use to judge someone else are going to be placed on the scale for us, as well. It is as though we judge and at the same time place the same bag of hopeless weights in the Lord's hands for us. We take away His prerogative and choose to live outside the Father's embrace. Worst of all, that scale in our hearts can never, never bring us close to God. We will be separated and find ourselves off in the corner somewhere, weighing our pain.

Consider the older brother in the story of the prodigal son.

> *"Now his older son was in the field, and when he came and approached the house, he heard music and dancing. And he summoned one of the servants and began inquiring what these things could be. And he said to him, 'Your brother has come, and your father has killed the fattened calf because he has received him back safe and sound.' But he became angry and was not willing to go in; and his father came out and began pleading with him. But he answered and said to his father, 'Look! For so many years I have been serving you and I have never neglected a command of yours; and yet you have never given me a young goat, so that I might celebrate with my friends; but when this son of yours came, who has devoured your wealth with prostitutes, you killed the fattened calf for him'"* (Luke 15:25-31).

This son is as separated from the Father as his younger, wayward brother was. This son had one of those "justice scales" in his heart, and he believed that he was ahead in the tally, even ahead of his father. This son's back is turned away from his father as much as his younger brother's was. He becomes angry because the scale seems to be tipped against him. He is trying to bring a fair balance. Notice the most frequent phases that are used by this older son: *"I have," "you have,"* and *"he has."* His relationships seem to have been determined by what he has or has done or what some other person can do for him.

Now, here is the tragedy of all this. This son was out in the field trying to earn what was already his—trying to find some kind of approval, making a name for himself, and trying to deserve the double portion that was his as the older son. And this son is as separated from his father's presence as the younger one was. Living with his eyes on "the scale," he cannot hear the voice of his father. He cannot even see his brother, and he cannot find the balance of peace.

The son's anger at the violation of his justice system kept him from going into the house and entering into celebration, and it kept him from the presence of his father, as well. Tragically, he missed the key word of the whole story, which is "brother." He says in effect, *"This son of yours ..."* This was his brother who was lost and had now come home. In his anger and insecurity he was unable to *see* his brother and only saw the scales upon which he weighed his worth. There was too much weight on the other end of the scale of this younger brother, too many offenses to be outweighed. He was ready to dismiss him and send him back to the pigpen.

Mercy makes us mad sometimes. Think of Jonah. I can hear him saying, "God, I knew you would show these pagan knuckleheads mercy. You are letting them off cheaply. All they have to do is repent. What about me and all the stuff I have put up with? I stink like bait from the inside of a fish just to bring your word of judgment. Now you took the weight of their sin off the scales just because they said they were sorry?! Well, I don't like it! Just go ahead and wipe me out. I don't get it." (See Jonah 4:1-3.)

Our internal scale of justice becomes our total focus and we cannot see anything else. The scale is a taskmaster that demands constant attention like an old coal furnace does. We are constantly having to tend the scale lest it become unbalanced and we are found wanting or we are called a fool. But we must remember that it is the foolish things that confound the wisdom of the world. (See 1 Corinthians 1:27.)

We will stop our balancing act only when something or someone sits down on the other end of the scale to justify us—to love us with a scandalous and glorious love. To shift the balance toward mercy: the weight of God's glory.

THE WEIGHT OF GLORY

Now the father opens his mouth and heart to this blind and distracted son:

> *"And he said to him, 'Son, you have always been with me, and all that is mine is yours. But we had to celebrate and*

rejoice, for this brother of yours was dead and has begun to live, and was lost and has been found'" (Luke 15:31, emphasis mine).

When the father says, *"Son, you have always been with me,"* the key word is "son."[1] He was a child of the father before he could hold a tool for work. This single word *child* outweighs all the works on the scale, whether they are good or evil. The father's agenda is to get the son back into the house and intimate communion—to cease from his preoccupation with the scale.

In that single, loving identification—"son"—the father draws all of his child's attention back to his face again. With that "sonship" comes all the weight of the father's goodness and treasure. The father is telling his child, "You have always been with me, even when you ignored me—even when you were distracted with worry and the scale. I have always remembered and longed to see your face. What is more, all that I have belongs to you so that you no longer have to turn away from me to earn it. I gave it to you long ago."

God is a righteous God, and there is, in fact, a scale that has to be balanced, but He has provided the weight himself for all who want to hear Him say, "son." He has not compromised His own holiness for our sake, but He has weighed all of our flops and sins and rebellion and placed a weight on the other end of the scale: His own Son, Jesus Christ.

"... nevertheless knowing that a man is not justified by the works of the Law but through faith in Christ Jesus, even we have believed in Christ Jesus, so that we may be justified by faith in Christ and not by the works of the Law; since by the works of the Law no flesh will be justified" (Gal. 2:16).

The Father has an agenda that includes the healing and restoration of anyone whose scales are hopelessly unbalanced. If that is His objective, it must then be ours as well. Our repentance is turning away from ourselves and our "scale of justice" and turning toward the face of the One who created us to live in intimate communion with Him and with one another.

Jesus said, "Be on your guard! If your brother sins, rebuke him; and if he repents, forgive him. And if he sins against you seven times a day, and returns to you seven times, saying, 'I repent,' forgive him." The apostles said to the Lord, "Increase our faith!" (Luke 17:3-5). In other words, we extend mercy to the penitent as often as it is needed. This answer blew the disciples away. They needed more faith, and so do we. They needed to trust the heart of God rather than the scales in their own hearts.

As with all of you, I have experienced my share of unfairness and even persecution at times. Once I felt that a man who was in authority over me betrayed me by speaking an untruth to the people I served in order to preserve the religious status quo. I will not guess at his motives for doing this. Suffice it to say that I was angry with this man and wanted to get out of ministry to these "crazy, hypocritical Christians." I had had it!

In the midst of my anger the Lord spoke sweetly that I needed to form a relationship with this leader, the one who I felt had betrayed me. I called the man and we arranged to meet for breakfast. Our first breakfast was a little tense for both of us, but we scheduled another. As we continued to meet together, the relationship grew until we were able to exchange books and thoughts. I began to pray for him and he prayed for me. I came to look forward to our breakfast meetings and other times when I would see him.

This man passed away a few years later and we never spoke of the original offense at any of our meetings. I had even ministered to his congregation and also to his leaders, and to him. I was given a gift by the grace of God in this relationship, as mercy triumphed over judgment once again.

The question, beloved, is not what is *fair*, but rather what is *necessary* to restore relationship. God's agenda is the healing of those who wound us. Can we trust the Lord enough to be covered in His mercy and then extend it to the ones who wound us? Remember that mercy costs us something—there is a divestment associated with it. Give your cloak, walk the mile, turn the cheek, and all of the above so as to extend mercy. Those who wrong you or wound you are not the enemy; the scale is the enemy!

The weights of our scales and justice system went crashing to the ground when Jesus was nailed to the cross just as they did when He upset the tables in the temple courtyard. We have made the "Father's house a place of business." (See John 2:16.) A greater glory and a great mercy are here in Jesus Christ, who sits on the other end of the scale because I need Him. Mercy is totally unreasonable and unfair. Bless God! It is nothing less than the weight of God's glory.

ENDNOTES

1 The Greek text uses the word *teknon*, best translated as "child."

Turning Points

FEEL THE PASSION

The scales have been tipped in our favor by the mercy of God who wants to see us face-to-face. Meditate on the following text by reading it to yourself several times aloud in a low tone until you can say it with your eyes closed. What is the Lord speaking to you?

> *He saved us, not on the basis of deeds...but according to His mercy...so that being justified by His grace we would be made heirs according to the hope of eternal life* (Titus 3:5-7, condensed to help you meditate on it more easily.).

Be sure to write down anything the Lord speaks to you in images, words, thoughts, or pictures.

What do the words and images that came to mind reveal to you about the heart of God. Write your observations here.

Now that you have received insights into the heart of God, what is He saying to you personally through His word? Take time to record your thoughts here.

EXPERIENCE THE PRESENCE

Beloved, the Lord has settled down on the other end of the scales with which you have judged your life and the lives of other folks. Allow yourself to come to a quiet place with Him and ask Him to reveal the weights you have placed on the scales of your own justice system. List those offenses, people, prejudices, etc., here and see the Lord sit at the other end of the scale. Let the bag of weights you have been carrying around your neck fall to the ground and be released forever.

SEE THE GLORY

Keep a careful eye on your heart in the coming days to identify any time when you place the weights of judgment on the scales either against yourself or someone else. Apply the weight of Christ's saving work to the scale and release offenses. List the times when you release weights in favor of grace.

CHAPTER 19

Seeds of Mercy

M y wife, Carol, and I, have lived in the small city of Chambersburg, Pennsylvania, for several years. We have enjoyed the warmth of the people in our town and its climate, as well. We have raised two girls here.

Chambersburg, in southeastern Pennsylvania, is surrounded by thousands of acres of apple and peach orchards. Often in the spring we drive through the apple orchards and enjoy the white or pink apple blossoms, and in the fall we smell the fragrance of the ripening fruits, which are ready for harvest.

When I hold an apple in my hand, I'm always amazed by the fact that each fruit has seeds within it, and those seeds become trees, and those trees produce more fruit, which has more seeds and so on. But it all springs from a single seed. Seeds produce fruit, and fruit produces more seeds.

Similarly, all life springs from a seed of some kind, whether it's a plant or an animal. This is the Creator's design. "God said, 'Let the earth sprout vegetation: plants yielding seed, and fruit trees on the earth bearing fruit after their kind with seed in them …'" (Gen. 1:11). Anything that is alive and reproduces does so through seeds of some kind, seeds that carry the DNA of the life that is being reproduced.

All life, even spiritual life, comes from a seed. It is not always easy to tell what kind of seed we are looking at, even when we hold it in our hands, until the seed is planted, dies, and produces its fruit. I can finally recognize what kind of seed has been planted by discovering what kind of fruit it produces. The fruit produced, therefore, is the glory of the seed.

THE FRUIT OF THE HEART

Our hearts are also filled with seeds and our lives are the produce or the fruit of those seeds. Jesus said, "… each tree is known by its own fruit…for his mouth speaks from that which fills his heart" (Luke 6:44-45). The fruit of the heart is what comes out of the mouth and into the life. We can see what kind of seed has been planted in our hearts by the fruit that is produced, the words and attitudes that express the seed in the world.

Every word we say plants some kind of seed in another heart. The words that have been spoken to you are seed-words. In the natural realm, if I plant apples in my orchard I should not be surprised to get apples during the harvest time. I can't plant peach seeds and expect to get apples. I will reap fruit according to the kind of seed that I've sown.

Thousands of little, seemingly innocuous events roll past our hearts, planting seeds that affect the rest of our days. As a dad, I get a little paranoid about what kinds of seeds I must have planted in the hearts of my own children. Our words and actions that we express in front of our children are seeds, and all of us have experienced and sown both good and bad seeds. Of course, we need not be healed of the good seeds, such as positive reinforcement and parental grace. All of us, like fertile seedbeds, have received mutated seeds that have produced distorted and defective fruit, which, in turn, contain more seeds that will be sown in future generations.

No other kind of fruit can be produced except that which comes from the seed sown in us, whether good or evil. Paul said, "Do not be deceived, God is not mocked; **for whatever a man sows, this he will also reap.** For the one who sows to his own **flesh** will from the flesh reap corruption, but the one who sows to the **Spirit** will from the Spirit reap eternal life" (Gal. 6:7-8, emphasis mine). Paul is making a simple point in this verse: Either my life is going to be pointed at myself or at the glory of God. One is the flesh and the other is the Spirit. As we sow to the Spirit, we produce the life or fruit of the Spirit, which is all about restoring and maintaining all kinds of relationships. If we sow to the flesh, on the other hand, it is all about us. The fruit of the Spirit is "love, joy, peace, patience, kindness, goodness, faithfulness, gentleness, self-control." (See Paul's contrast between the flesh and the Spirit in Galatians 5:14-26.) A seed of the flesh or mere justice germinates as glory to us, whereas seeds of the Spirit bring glory to God.

We know what kind of seed has been planted by the fruit it produces. Seeds and their subsequent fruit can be heard as they are passed from parent to child and from generation to generation like a native dialect. There may be a seed of shame, for example, which brings forth a dialect of condescension. A seed of disrespect for women will produce a fruit of abuse. For instance, if a little girl grows up in a home filled with anger and profanity, she will probably not speak like Mary Poppins. The fruits that are obvious are the words and attitudes of our hearts and the actions we exhibit.

I will let you in on a little "trade secret." Many times I can tell what kind of seed was planted in the heart of someone I am talking to by the way they make me feel when I am in their presence. I travel to many churches as part of my ministry. If I walk into a church and begin to straighten my tie (assuming I have to wear one, which I hate to do), then I may be picking up something like shame. If I see a congregation where folks tend to stick to themselves in small pockets, they may be producing or experiencing the fruit of rejection or insecurity.

A few years back, a man who had "a little problem" with anger was brought to my home. He had just torn the front door off of his house! When I greeted him at the back door, I found a man who was about six-feet, three-inches tall. He was wearing earrings and his body was covered with tattoos. Obviously, he was a "biker dude," and I must admit I felt a little afraid of him. I felt like I needed to make sure I had an escape plan if things didn't go well.

As I ministered to this huge man, we found hidden deep within him a three-year-old little boy whose stepfather had terrorized him by locking him in a phone booth in the middle of the hot summer, an act that might have killed him. The stepfather also beat up his mom in a drunken rage while the little boy pounded with his fists helplessly at the man's leg. Seeds of fear had been planted in this child's heart, which would yield the fruit of fear for his own family and children forty years later.

What was amazing was that when the man found healing for this fear, his countenance completely changed The seed that had been sown was uprooted and replaced with seeds of compassion, which brought forth grace and mercy. The man's wife and children followed him by receiving their healing, and new seed was being sown for generations to come. The principle is still true: whatever is in your heart is going to come out into your life. Seeds of compassion had replaced the fear. The question we must consider is this: What kind of fruit do we want to harvest from the hearts around us?

UPROOTING AND REPLANTING SEEDS OF MERCY

In our years of living in this orchard region we have witnessed an eerie sight from time to time. When an orchard's trees are diminishing in their yield, the orchardists uproot older trees, sometimes in huge areas at a time. I recall on several occasions driving by one of these uprooted orchards with their trees laying on their sides and the exposed roots jutting into the air. It looked like something out of a Hitchcock movie. Once the old trees are uprooted, the orchardists must come back and replant trees from new stock, which in turn bear more fruit for generations to come.

If we are to produce new fruit, we must also uproot and remove old seeds that produce little or bad fruit. The same principle that Jesus stated regarding the abundance of our hearts and words also works for us when we replant new seeds. We can replant new seeds and replace them with kingdom seeds. Through forgiveness and mercy we plant new words/seeds.

As we bless those who have offended us, an exchange takes place through mercy.

> *To sum up, all of you be harmonious, sympathetic, brotherly, kindhearted, and humble in spirit; not returning evil*

for evil or insult for insult, but giving a blessing instead; for you were called for the very purpose that you might inherit a blessing (1 Pet. 3:8-9).

See that no one repays another with evil for evil, but always seek after that which is good for one another and for all people. (1 Thess. 5:15).

Beloved, we must consider what is *needed* rather than what is *deserved* if we are to give glory to God. Our Father seldom gives us what we deserve, and that is a very good thing. We need to move from asking what is fair or what feels good or right on a human level and begin to ask what we would like to sow and reap in the hearts of others, even those who have wounded or mistreated us.

There is an exchange of seed that takes place in our hearts when we turn toward mercy. Just as Jesus spoke the principle that our hearts produce the fruit of whatever is planted in them, when we speak out of a heart of compassion, we are planting seeds of compassion. When we are healed, the fear or other wounding is replaced with compassion and then we speak out of compassion to the one who wounded us in the first place. *Until what is in our hearts has been replaced with compassion, we are not healed!*

I sat with a woman for a few healing prayer sessions and discovered that her mother had terribly abused her. Seeds of abuse and shame had been planted in her life, and they had brought forth the unpleasant fruit of anger and hatred. As the Lord continued to bring healing to her, I encouraged the woman to allow the Lord to see the heart of her mother who had wounded her.

During our encounter with the presence of God, I asked the Lord to remind her of areas of blessing for her mother. Immediately the Lord began to pour out a stream of positive memories in which the mother had blessed her daughter through things like making her favorite foods for her birthday or buying her pretty dresses and other special times they had shared. As the flood of these memories continued, the daughter was able to pray blessing on her mother and, as she did so, her heart softened and all the hatred was absorbed in compassion. As she blessed her mother, her own healing happened.

She was able to forgive in greater release and to see her mother with compassion. We will never totally forgive or release anyone until we see them as the Father sees them, thereby allowing our hearts to be filled with compassion for them.

Jesus was faithful to produce the seed that had been placed in His heart by the Husbandman. He never operated from any other basis, and His constant concern was to bring glory to the Father.

I am afraid the church herself is producing fruit that points to the seed. There has been an emphasis over the past few decades on what God will do *for me* rather than what He might do *in or through me*. This is a seed in the flesh. What is begun in the flesh will not produce anything in the Spirit to the glory of God. Why are we surprised when we see leaders who fall into adultery and other forms of immorality? They are simply reproducing the seed that has been sown in their lives.

The church has also germinated seeds of shame and religion. There is little or no difference between controlling, shaming religious attitudes and sexual immorality. This is because in both cases there is an absence of mercy.

We are an apostate people who produce the glory of the flesh rather than expose the glory of God, which is His mercy. We must sow in mercy in order to see the world turning toward mercy and the heart of the Father. The chief question becomes: what do you want to plant in the other person's heart? The way to be free of religion, anger, judgment, and all the rest is to replace these things with a new seed: compassion. We must set our minds and motives on the Spirit. "For the **mind set on the flesh is death,** but the **mind set on the Spirit is life and peace**" (Rom. 8:6).

THE ULTIMATE SEED

Seeds and fruit were among the final word pictures Jesus painted before He went to the cross. As Jesus and His close friends and disciples walked eastward across the valley to Gethsemane and the final showdown with the power of sin and the devil, they would have encountered grapevines all around them.

Speaking in plain and pictorial language, Jesus said, "I am the vine, you are the branches. He who abides in Me, and I in him, bears much fruit; for without Me you can do nothing" (John 15:5, NKJV). Here Jesus was speaking of seeds and fruit.

Jesus is the ultimate Seed of the Father's DNA. This was the Father's intention all along, as He revealed His heart prophetically through the Psalmist:

> *I have made a covenant with My chosen;*
> *I have sworn to David My servant,*
> *I will establish your seed forever*
> *And build up your throne to all generations.*
> (Ps. 89:3-4)

Jesus was the Seed of the Father's life that was sown at the cross. He was the express image of the Father, and He had the same heart as His Father. When we see Jesus, we see the Father. Jesus said, "He who has seen Me has seen the Father" (John 14:9). What the Father was the Son was also. Jesus planted no seed of His own, only what was in the Father's heart.

Jesus spent at least three years planting seeds that were given by the Father, the "Husbandman" of the vine—demonstrating and revealing mercy. Jesus was "The Word (who) became flesh, and dwelt among us, and we saw His glory, glory as of the only begotten from the Father, full of grace and truth" (John 1:14). He was a seedpod filled—bursting with the seed of Heaven's life—the very glory and expression of the divine instinct.

Mercy had to be demonstrated for the heart of the Father to be revealed in the earth.

Mercy is all about intimacy and restoration, "faces-to-faces." I suppose it's theoretically possible that Jesus could have covered our sin by simply submitting to death on the cross. That would have been power over sin and death, but it would not have been power for life. Jesus did much more: He planted seeds of heaven's life in us—the DNA of the Father's heart, which is filled with *compassion*, overflowing in *grace*, and revealed through *mercy*.

The Father's awesome heart of compassion had to be sown in the hearts of men, and the only way that could happen was for Jesus to come and demonstrate the Father's glory, which is His mercy. Mercy must be *shown* if it is to be seen and transplanted into the hearts of men—if heaven is going to be established on earth.

Jesus was the "Seed" of the Father's life, but that Seed had to die in order to germinate and bring forth more life. "...unless a grain of wheat falls into the earth and dies, it remains alone; but if it dies, it bears much fruit" (John 12:24). The Lord of glory allowed Himself to be sown as a seed of mercy, bringing glory to the Father and bringing us back to Him again.

Jesus, like Moses, was issued an invitation to come up to a higher life and to bring us with Him. Jesus responded to the ultimate invitation of the Father and brought heaven to earth, "so that Christ may dwell in [our] hearts through faith; and that [we], being rooted and grounded in love, may be able to comprehend with all the saints what is the breadth and length and height and depth, and to know the love of Christ which surpasses knowledge, that [we] may be filled up to all the fullness of God" (Eph. 3:17-19, pronouns changed).

Turning Points

FEEL THE PASSION

What is the Lord speaking to your heart? He wants to plant and cultivate seeds of mercy for you and through you. Meditate on the following scripture verse by reading it to yourself several times until you can say it with your eyes closed. What kinds of thoughts, images, words, or pictures come to your mind?

> *"For you have been born again not of seed which is perishable but imperishable, that is, through the living and enduring word of God"* (1 Pet. 1:23).

Given the words and images you have received, what is the Lord speaking to you about Himself? Write your thoughts and insights here.

The Lord has been communicating a personal word to you through the *logos* and the images that came to mind. What do you now hear Him speaking to your heart? Write it down here.

EXPERIENCE THE PRESENCE

Valued one, seeds have been invested in your life from many sources. They were the words and wounds of those around you. The words and seeds that you received came from people who had no other kind of seeds but those that they themselves had received.

Allow yourself to come to a safe and quiet place in the Lord and ask Him to reveal unmerciful seeds that have been planted in your heart. They were the words that left a mark on you. Ask Him then to reveal how you may have passed those words and seeds along to others including the ones you love. Make two lists below, one for each of these seeds either gotten or given.

SEE THE GLORY

Watch your words and attitudes in the coming days to keep track of the seeds you are sowing. Observe the attitudes and words of those around you as well and the fruit they produce in you. Record your observations here.

CHAPTER 20

The Brilliant Darkness

WHEN THE SIXTH HOUR CAME, DARKNESS FELL OVER THE WHOLE LAND UNTIL THE NINTH HOUR. AT THE NINTH HOUR JESUS CRIED OUT WITH A LOUD VOICE, "ELOI, ELOI, LAMA SABACHTHANI" WHICH IS TRANSLATED, "MY GOD, MY GOD, WHY HAVE YOU FORSAKEN ME" (MARK 15:33–34).

The invitation had been engraved before anything was spoken into being. Before the eternal breath was exhaled to form the first man, a mountain could be seen in the distance. The same breath that formed the man uttered a bittersweet invitation from the mountain, "*Come up here...*" Through thousands of years of heartbreak and scorned overtures, the eternal face, the Christ of God, was set like flint toward the mountain and the invitation that fluttered in the heart of God.

This Son was the manifested face of His Father. "We look at this Son and see the God who cannot be seen. We look at this Son and see God's original purpose in everything created. For everything, absolutely everything, above and below, visible and invisible, rank after rank after rank of angels—everything got started in Him and finds its purpose in Him. He was there before any of it came into existence and holds it all together right up to this moment" (Colossians 1:15-17, MSG).

And now, in the next eternal instant, the Lamb, the sinless offering of the Father's heart, was mutilated beyond recognition and led through the streets in plain view of the world, with the mountain now before him. His steps labored up the mountain and disappeared in the heart of the Father. And when the procession of death stopped, the eternal face of God was nailed to a rough-hewn cross and lifted up from the earth in suffocating agony. Naked and not ashamed, He began to declare the very theme of His journey back to the Father, *"Forgive them ... have mercy ..."*

Now it was at the sixth hour and a picture was forming in the spirit realm. The Source of life was bound to this revisited tree of knowledge, the source of all death. When the sun was at its apex, a spiritual darkness began its silent, creeping assault upon Calvary, the Mount of Invitation. All natural light was filtered out and darkness shrouded the Face. Now, flanking the cross upon which the Eternal Face was suspended between heaven and earth, two gigantic cherubim could be seen in the spirit extending their wings over this cruel emblem of human shame. Calvary became a *mercy seat*, and the Lamb became the at-*one*-ment of God. At once there was a natural darkness and a glorious spiritual, golden brilliance.

In the brilliant darkness that now connected heaven and earth, the Face could find no other to meet His. He spoke in a labored gasp, out of the empty, vacuous air, as the weight of humanity and the separation from the Father erupted, *"Father, why have you forsaken me?"* With that, the eternal breath was given up and returned to the Source.

In that place of darkness all movement and religion with its detached human effort became useless. This was the ultimate act of selflessness and the fullest expression of the Father's heart and exposition of His mercy. This was the outpouring of the Father's wrath upon the Son in whom He delighted. Sin was laid upon Him and the cross became a scale—the scale upon which the righteousness of God was satisfied and the heart of the Father was broken.

In that ultimate, embracing darkness the emblems and heart of the *mercy seat* were fulfilled in this scene of misery and gore. This was the exposition of the *passion*, the *presence*, and the *glory* of the Father's heart.

The crown of gold became a crown of thorns upon the eternal brow. The purple robe was laid aside and divided among those who murdered the Son of God. As the Mount of Invitation lay under the overshadowing wings of the cherubim, Calvary became the throne of unreasonable love. Under that shadow, in the place of intimate embrace, all religious effort and movement stopped and we were again connected with the womb of the Father's love for us. Now man could stop trying to be good enough and begin to respond to the goodness of God.

Once again, the Lord Jesus at Calvary reaches out His hands to present the people back to the Father and put everything back in order.

> "... *everything of God finds its proper place in him without crowding. Not only that, but all the broken and dislocated pieces of the universe—people and things, animals and atoms—get properly fixed and fit together in vibrant harmonies, all because of his death, his blood that poured down from the Cross. You yourselves are a case study of what he does. At one time you all had your backs turned to God, thinking rebellious thoughts of him, giving him trouble every chance you got. But now, by giving himself completely at the Cross, actually dying for you, Christ brought you over to God's side and put your lives together, whole and holy in His presence*" (Colossians 1:19-22, MSG).

Now at the last moment, the Son returned the breath of creation to the Father and said, "*It is accomplished!*"

ON EARTH AS IT IS IN HEAVEN

What was accomplished in that powerful demonstration of the Father's resolve and affection was a shifting of focus to the face and the throne of the One who created us. In the Old Testament the Father *revealed* the mercy seat. In Christ He *became* a mercy seat. Now, in these days, the Lord is forming His mercy seat in you and me, where the will and heart of heaven flow to the earth through us. Consider the words of Jesus:

> *Again I say unto you, that if two of you shall agree on earth as touching any thing that they shall ask, it shall be done for them of my Father which is in heaven. For where two or three are gathered together in my name, there am **I in the midst of them*** (Matt. 18:19-20, KJV, emphasis mine).

When I close my eyes to *see* this scripture, I see the mercy seat of God. Recall the very beginning of this writing and the Book of Exodus when two cherubim were *turned toward mercy*. (See Exodus 25:20.) The cherubim in the scriptures indicate the presence of God. Jesus teaches us now of a new order of cherubim: *Us!* As I see Jesus' words to us, there are two cherubim who agree as if they arched their touching wings. They are turned toward each other and toward the mercy seat. Now, instead of wings, we bring the needy to the secret place, under the shadow of the wings on the mercy seat and set our hearts to bring them to healing. Mercy is of God and wherever mercy is, God is. As we turn our hearts toward mercy, we become the presence of the living God and the heirs of Christ Jesus. We represent the passion, become the Presence, and show forth the glory of God.

Through the work of Christ in that brilliant darkness of Calvary, we have nothing left to prove and all superfluous religious movement stops. As we shift our focus away from ourselves and toward the mercy of God for healing and restoration, we proclaim that "The kingdom of God has come near to you" (Luke 10: 9).

Beloved one, be filled with the breath of God and let His mercy do its re-creative work in and through you. See those broken and lifeless ones at the side of the road and wrap the life of the Father around them. Allow the Holy Spirit to fill your lungs as you breathe encouragement to them and praise to the Father's love. Then the knowledge of the glory of the Lord will cover the earth as waters cover the sea when we all *turn toward mercy*. (See Hab. 2:14.)

FEEL THE PASSION

We are called to become the *mercy seat* of God, filled with mercy—the *passion*, the *presence*, and the *glory* of God. Meditate on the scripture below and allow the Lord to speak to you personally through words, thoughts, images, or whatever other means He chooses.

> *"Again I say unto you, that if two of you shall agree on earth as touching any thing that they shall ask, it shall be done for them of my Father which is in heaven. For where two or three are gathered together in my name, there am **I in the midst of them**"* (Matt. 18:19-20, KJV, emphasis mine).

Be sure to write down what the Lord is speaking to you as you meditate on the scriptures.

What do these words and images reveal to you about the heart of God? Write your insights here.

Given all the Lord has revealed about Himself to you through the words and images you received, what is He speaking to you personally? What is your personal revelation now of the heart of God toward you? Write His personal word here.

EXPERIENCE THE PRESENCE

Greatly loved one, you are called to become the *mercy seat* of God filled with mercy, the *passion*, the *presence* and the *glory* of God. He has done all that is necessary, settled all the accounts and closed the chasm between your heart and His, not to mention your heart and the hearts of any who have offended you.

Experience the presence of God as you look at the cross of Christ: the ultimate mercy seat of God. As you stand there at the foot of the cross allow the blood of Christ to be applied to any and all remaining wounds, injustices or offenses. Turn your heart toward the cross. Allow the comforting darkness of Calvary to settle over you now — to absorb and overwhelm religion and mere justice. Turn your heart toward mercy.

Write any thoughts that come to mind as you meditate on your being hidden in Christ. Is there anything that you have not brought to the ultimate mercy seat?

SEE THE GLORY

We have spent this entire book turning toward the mercy of God. Look back at all the previous chapters where you have been giving glory to God and now write a summary of them. How has your life and heart now been turned toward mercy?